FIRST SCHOOL PRIZE

Presented to

Mary English
NAME OF STUDENT

Blenheim District High School
SCHOOL

for

Senior Essay
CATEGORY

SENIOR SECTION

★

June 1, 1961.
DATE

R. A. Cruickshank B.A.
PRINCIPAL'S SIGNATURE

Brooke Bond
TRAVEL AND EDUCATIONAL AWARDS

A SPECIAL EDITION
FOR YOUNG READERS

The Sea around Us

by Rachel Carson

ADAPTED BY

ANNE TERRY WHITE

GOLDEN PRESS

NEW YORK

ACKNOWLEDGMENTS

The illustrations for this book could not have been assembled without the cooperation and courtesy of a great many persons and institutions. Where our obligations can be specifically acknowledged, they appear in the list below:

American Potash & Chemical Corporation: p. 143

Arabian-American Oil Company: p. 144

Ray Atkeson: p. 101

Canadian National Railways: p. 123 (top)

Stevan Celebonovic: pp. 15, 18, 84 (bottom)

Compania Mexicana Aerofoto, S.A.: p. 142

Howell Conant/Topix: p. 61

H. L. Consley: 5 (bottom), 128 (bottom), 129

Culver Service: p. 121

Walt Disney Studios: p. 123 (bottom)

European: p. 93

N. R. Farbman: p. 119

Andreas Feininger: pp. 14, 87

Fouke Fur Company: pp. 32-33

Ewing Galloway: cover, pp. 84 (top), 105

Fritz Goro: pp. 7, 20, 25, 28, 29, 42, 46, 80, 82-83, 102, 106, 112, 128 (top), 130, 131 (bottom), 140, 141, 163

Carola Gregor: pp. 94-95

Esther Henderson/Rapho Guillumette: p. 115

Robert C. Hermes: p. 100

Dr. H. H. Hess: p. 58

Motoi Kumai: p. 96

Dr. David Lack and the California Academy of Science: p. 78

Lamont Geophysical Observatory: p. 65

Cy La Tour: p. 19

Lt. Alan Lisle: p. 70

Laurence Lowry/A. Devaney: p. 98

Laurence Lowry/Rapho Guillumette: p. 52

R. F. McAllister: pp. 56, 57

Macmillan & Co. Ltd.: p. 40

Norwegian National Travel Office: p. 88

Peabody Institute Library, Baltimore: p. 148

R. T. Peterson/National Audubon: p. 30 (top)

Rutherford Platt: pp. 4 (middle, bottom), 68, 117, 131 (top), 134, 135, 137, 158

Jean Roubier/Rapho Guillumette: p. 154

Royal Geographical Society: p. 159

Dr. Robert Sharp: p. 86

Warren Shearman and *American Heritage*: p. 146

Standard Oil Co. (N.J.): pp. 49, 51, 139, 145

Unesco—IUCN/Eibl-Eibesfeldt: p. 79, 113

United States Air Force: p. 75 (bottom)

Dr. Roman Vishniac: pp. 11-13, 23, 124

Cole Weston/Rapho Guillumette: endpapers, p. 89

Wide World: p. 103

Dr. Douglas Wilson: pp. 30 (bottom), 31, 33 (bottom)

S. C. Wilson: pp. 5 (top), 122, 149

Woods Hole Oceanographic Institution: p. 48

The chart of the North Atlantic on pp. 160-161 is from Chart 1400 of the Hydrographic Office of the United States Navy.

The quotation from Dr. Robert Cushman Murphy on p. 115 is from "The Askoy Expedition," in *Natural History* (1944, p. 356), reproduced by permission.

ILLUSTRATIONS BY
RENE MARTIN
MAPS BY
EMIL LOWENSTEIN

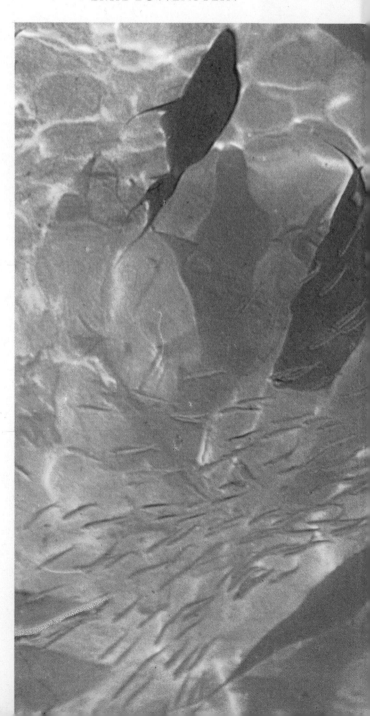

Contents

The Gray Beginnings

BEGINNINGS are often shadowy, and so it is with the beginnings of that great mother of life, the sea. Many people have debated how and when the earth acquired its ocean, and it is not surprising that their explanations do not always agree. The truth is that no one was there to see. So if I tell here the story of how the young planet Earth came to have an ocean, it must be a story pieced from many sources and cemented together with imagination. The story is founded on the testimony of the earth's most ancient rocks, on evidence written on the face of the moon, and on hints contained in the story of the sun and the stars. For although no man was there to witness the birth of the sea, the stars and the moon and the rocks were there. Indeed, they had much to do with the fact that there is an ocean.

The events of which I write must have happened more than three billion years ago. For that is about how old the earth is, and the ocean must be very nearly as old. The new earth, freshly torn from the sun, was a ball of whirling gases, intensely hot. Gradually the flaming gases cooled. They began to liquefy, and Earth became a molten mass.

The materials of this mass sorted themselves out according to weight: the heaviest in the center, the less heavy ones surrounding them, and the least heavy forming the outer rim. This is the pattern that persists today. The center of the earth is a ball of molten iron, very nearly as hot as it was three billion years ago. Around it is a middle layer, not fully hardened, of a dark rock known as basalt. Beyond that is a hard outer shell, relatively thin and made up of solid basalt and granite.

The outer shell of the young earth must have been a good many million years changing from the liquid to the solid state. And it is believed by some that, before this change was completed, an event of the greatest importance took place—the moon was formed. We all know that the moon draws the tides. But the next time you stand on the beach at night, watching the moon's bright path across the water, remember this: the moon itself may have been born of a great tidal wave, not of water but of earthly material, torn off into space. And if so, the event had much to do with shaping the ocean basins and the continents.

There were tides in the new earth long before there was an ocean. They were tides of molten rock. The pull of the sun raised these rock tides over the earth's whole surface, and they rolled without stopping around the globe.

Now those who believe that the moon is a child of earth say that, owing to certain forces, these tides of earthly material drawn by the sun kept getting steadily higher and faster. Finally those on the side towards the sun became too high, and a great wave was torn away and hurled into space. But immediately, of course, this newly created moon was affected by the forces that control moving objects and went spinning in its own path around the earth.

There are reasons for believing that this event took place after the earth's crust had become slightly hardened. For there is to this day a great scar on the face of the globe. This scar or depression holds the Pacific Ocean. Can it be the moon scar? The floor of the Pacific, according to some scientists, is composed of basalt, which is the stuff of the earth's middle layer, whereas all other oceans are floored with a thin layer of granite. We immediately wonder: What became of the Pacific's granite covering? The most convenient answer is that it may have been torn away when the moon was formed. The moon itself tells us something that supports the theory. It is much less dense than the earth. This suggests that the moon took away none of the earth's heavy iron core, but is made up only of the granite and some of the basalt of the outer layers.

When the moon was born there was no ocean. There was only a scar which one day would hold an ocean. Around the gradually cooling earth were heavy layers of cloud. They contained much of the water of the new planet. For a long time the earth's surface was so hot that no moisture could fall without immediately being changed to steam. The dense covering of clouds was continually renewed and must have been very thick. No rays of sunlight could penetrate it. So the rough outlines of the continents and the empty ocean basins were sculptured out of the surface of the earth in darkness, in a world of heated rock and swirling clouds and gloom.

As soon as the earth's crust cooled enough, the rains began to fall. Never have there been such

rains since that time. They fell continuously, day and night, days passing into months, into years, into centuries. They poured into the waiting basins. Or, falling upon the continents, they drained away to become sea.

That earliest ocean must have been only faintly salt. But from the moment the rains began to fall, the lands began to be worn away. The minerals in the rocks dissolved and were carried with the rock fragments to the ocean. This process has gone on and on without pause. And over the eons of time the sea has grown ever more bitter with the salt of the continents.

In what manner the sea produced the mysterious and wonderful stuff called protoplasm, of which all living things are made, we cannot say. In the warm, dimly lit waters of that early sea, the temperature and pressure and saltiness must have been exactly right to bring about the creation of life from materials that were not alive. We do not know just what these conditions were, and chemists have been unable to duplicate them in their laboratories.

Before the first living cell was created—perhaps several billion years ago—there may have been many trials and failures. It seems probable that there were several steps along the way. Perhaps

The earliest plants and animals must have been simpler even than this diatom, a one-celled plant that is common in waters near our shores today.

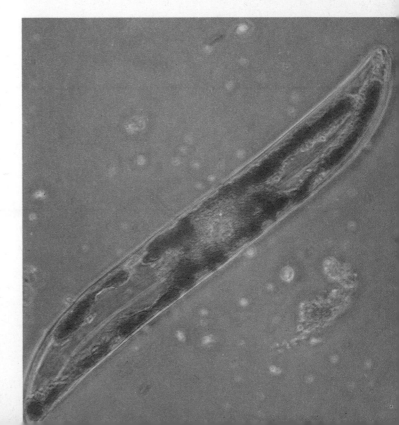

◄ *For billions of years the moon has accompanied the earth on its journey through space, drawing the earth's seas toward it in the rhythmic surge of tides.*

the complex molecules of protoplasm arose from these in-between forms. Perhaps these molecules somehow became able to reproduce themselves and to grow together, and so to begin the endless stream of life. But at present no one is wise enough to be sure.

Those first living things may have been like some of the bacteria we know today—mysterious borderline forms that were not quite plants, not quite animals. They may have been just barely over the line that separates the non-living from the living. Probably these first children of the sea fed on the carbon compounds then present in the ocean waters. Or, like the iron and sulfur bacteria that exist today, they lived directly on the minerals present in the sea.

All the while the cloud cover was getting thinner and thinner, and finally the sun for the first time shone through upon the earth. By this time some of the living things that floated in the sea must have developed the magic of chlorophyll, the green coloring matter by means of which plants in sunlight make their food. Now they were able to take the carbon dioxide of the air and the water of the sea and make them over into the starches

This Lichmophora diatom (below) and the radiolarian (above) are part of the life of our present seas.

and sugars and other substances they needed for life. So the first true plants came into being.

Another group of living things, having no chlorophyll, found they could make a way of life for themselves by devouring the plants. So the first animals arose, and from that day to this, every animal in the world has followed the habit it learned in the ancient seas. Directly or indirectly it depends on the plants for food and life.

As the years passed, and the millions of years, life grew more and more complex. From simple, one-celled creatures, others arose that were collections of cells. Then came creatures with organs for feeding, digesting, breathing, reproducing. Sponges grew on the rocky bottom of the sea's edge and coral animals built their homes in warm, clear waters. Jellyfish swam and drifted in the sea. Worms developed, and starfish, and hard-shelled creatures with many-jointed legs, the arthropods.

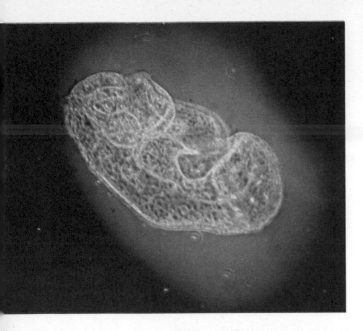

The plants, too, progressed, from microscopic algae to seaweeds with rootlike holdfasts to grip the rocks as they swayed in the tides.

During all this time the continents had no life. Indeed, there was little to encourage living things to come ashore. Imagine a continent of bleak, naked rock, a continent without soil, a land silent except for the sound of the rains and winds that swept across it! For there was no living voice, and no living thing moved over its surface.

Meanwhile the planet was gradually getting cooler. The outer layers had been the first to cool. Now, as the interior cooled and contracted, it drew away from the outer shell. This shell was now too big, and in order to fit the shrinking earth, the

Even the smallest animals of the sea can be highly developed, and quite different one from the next—witness the 14-day-old starfish larva (above, left), the Beak Thrower (above, right), and the larvae of the sea urchin (below, left) and of the horseshoe crab.

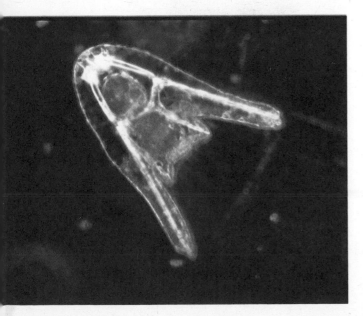

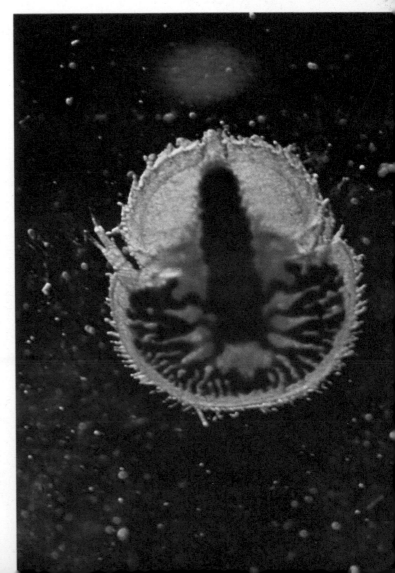

crust fell into folds and wrinkles—the first mountain ranges.

Geologists tell us that those first mountains have long since been worn away. So have the ranges that immediately followed them. Then about a billion years ago came a third great period of mountain building, and of those majestic mountains we have two reminders today. They are the Laurentian hills of eastern Canada and a great shield of granite over the flat country around Hudson Bay.

There was still no plant covering over the earth. But life continued to develop in the sea. The earliest forms have left no fossils to tell us what creatures they were. Probably they were soft-bodied, with no hard parts that could be preserved. But even if they had had hard parts, they would have left no traces of their existence. For the rock layers formed in those early days have since been so changed by enormous heat and pressure that such fossils as they might have contained would have been destroyed.

For the past 500 million years, however, the rocks have kept the record of life by preserving the fossil remains. Five hundred million years ago life in the sea, the fossils tell us, had already progressed very far. All the main groups of animals without a backbone had been developed. But there were no animals with backbones, no insects or spiders. And there was still no plant or animal that could venture onto the forbidding land. So for at least three-fourths of the time that life has existed on the planet, the continents lay silent and

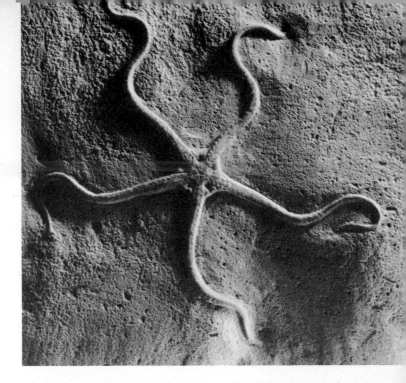

Though starfish have changed greatly, this fossil of 150 million years ago is still recognizable to us.

uninhabited, while the sea prepared the life that was later to invade them. Meanwhile, with violent tremblings of the earth and with the fire and smoke of roaring volcanoes, mountains rose and wore away, glaciers moved to and fro over the earth, and the sea crept over the continents and again withdrew.

It was not until some 350 million years ago that the first pioneer of land life crept out on the shore. It was an arthropod, one of the great tribe from which, later on, crabs and lobsters and insects came. It must have been something like a modern

These Cretaceous fishes, now confined in the Paris Museum of Natural History, once roamed the seas in the region that is now Lebanon. ▶

Of the trilobites that once swarmed over the shores only fossils now remain— but in their larval stage the horseshoe crabs of today ◀ *(p. 13) still resemble them.*

scorpion, but it lived a strange life, half on land, half in water, something like that of the ghost crabs that speed along the beaches today and now and then dash into the surf to moisten their gills.

Fish now appeared in the rivers. In times of drought, when there was a shortage of oxygen in the drying pools and lagoons, the fish developed swim bladders for the storage of air.

It is doubtful that the animals alone would have succeeded in colonizing the land. For only the plants had the power to improve its first harsh conditions. They helped to make soil of the crumbling rocks. They held back the soil from the rains that would have washed it away. We know very little about the first land plants, but they must have been much like some of the larger seaweeds which had developed stronger stems and rootlike holdfasts to resist the drag and pull of the surf in shallow waters. Perhaps in some low lands along the coast, from which the sea often drained away, such plants found it possible to survive even though they were separated from the water.

The earth's third mountain ranges gradually wore away. Rain and wind and frost and air crumbled them into fragments, and the rivers carried away the fragments and deposited them in the lowlands. The weight of this rock waste was so great that vast areas of the continent sank under it. And as they sank, the seas crept out of their basins and spread over the lands.

Life fared well in those shallow, sunlit seas. But when later on the lands rose again and the seas retreated, many creatures must have been left stranded in the shallow, landlocked bays. Some of these animals found means to get along on land. One was a strange fishlike creature, and over the thousands of years its fins became legs, and instead of gills it developed lungs. And so, in Devonian

ARCHEOZOIC

PROTEROZOIC

PALEOZOIC

16

Conditions on earth changed many times during the successive eras shown below. It is amid these changes in the environment that life evolved from the earliest living cells to the plants and animals we know today.

CENOZOIC

MESOZOIC

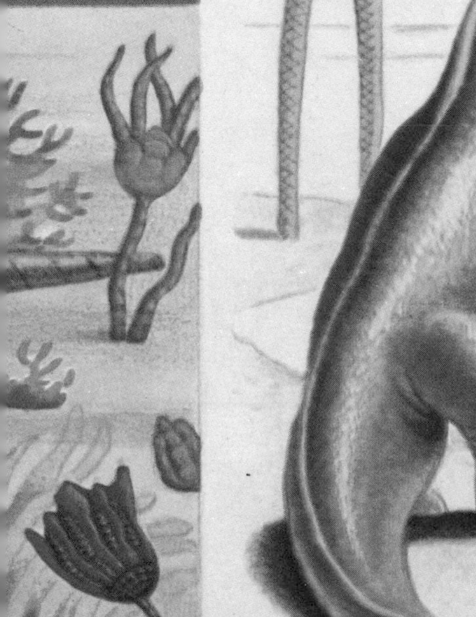

17

sandstone, we have found the footprint of the first amphibian, the ancestor of frogs and salamanders.

On land and sea the stream of life poured on. On land, mosses and ferns and seed plants developed. The reptiles for a time dominated the earth —gigantic, terrifying. Birds learned to move in the air. The first small mammals lurked in crannies of the earth as though in fear of the reptiles.

When they went ashore, the animals that took up a land life carried with them a part of the sea in their bodies, a heritage which even today links each land animal with the ancient sea. Each of us carries in our veins a salty stream in which the elements sodium, potassium, and calcium are combined in almost the same proportions as in sea water. This has come down to us from the day, millions of years ago, when a far-off ancestor developed a circulatory system in which the fluid was merely the water of the sea. In the same way the protoplasm that makes up each cell of our bodies has the same chemical structure as that of the first simple creatures that arose in the ancient sea.

Time seems to have arrested the flight of this pterodactyl. It lingers on, in the form of this fossil, to tell us of the evolution of birds from reptiles.

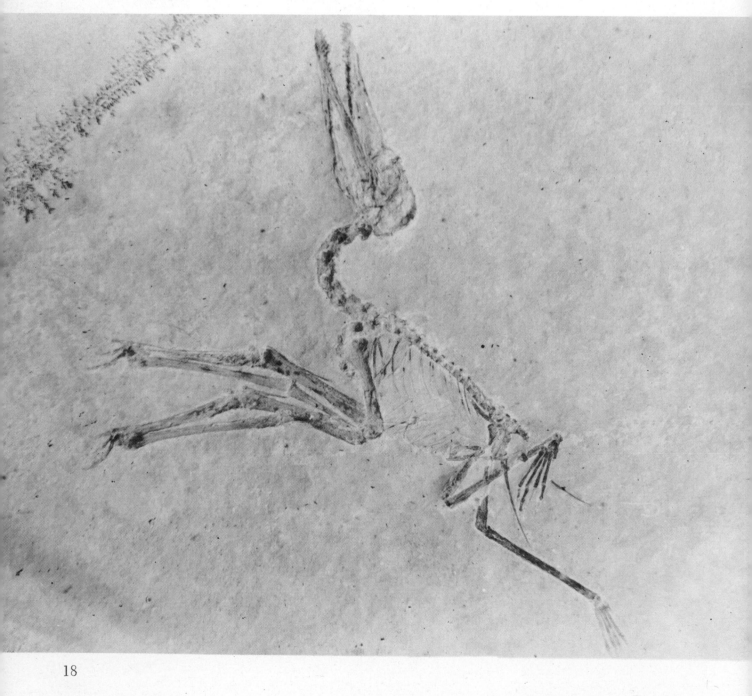

Some of the land animals later returned to the ocean. After perhaps 50 million years of life on land, a number of reptiles entered the sea. They were huge creatures. Some had oarlike limbs; some were web-footed, with long, serpentlike necks. These monsters disappeared millions of years ago, but we remember them when we come upon a large sea turtle swimming many miles out at sea. Much later some of the mammals, too, abandoned a land life for the ocean. Their descendants are the sea lions, seals, and whales of today.

Among the land mammals there was a race of creatures that took to the trees. Their hands became skilled in picking up and handling objects, and along with this skill came a superior brain power. At last, perhaps somewhere in the vast interior of Asia, they came down from the trees and became again ground creatures. The past million years have seen their transformation into beings with the body and brain and spirit of man.

Eventually man, too, found his way back to the sea. He could not physically re-enter it as the seals and whales had done. But over the centuries, with all the ingenuity of his mind, he has sought to explore and investigate its most remote parts, so that he might re-enter it imaginatively.

He fashioned boats to venture out on its surface. Later he found ways to descend to the shallow parts of its floor, carrying with him the air that he needed to breathe. He found ways to probe its depths, he let down nets to capture its life, he invented mechanical eyes and ears that could re-create for his senses a world long lost.

In the wondering eyes of this little tarsier we may read the history of man's not very distant ancestors.

And yet he has returned to his mother sea only on her own terms. He cannot control or change the ocean as he has subdued and plundered the continents. In the artificial world of his cities and towns, he often forgets the true nature of his planet and its long history in which man has occupied a mere moment of time. The sense of all these things comes to him most clearly in the course of a long ocean voyage, when day after day he watches the horizon, ridged and furrowed by waves; when at night he becomes aware of the turning of the earth as the stars pass overhead; or when alone in this world of water and sky, he feels the loneliness of his earth in space. And then he knows that his world is a water world, a planet dominated by its covering mantle of ocean, in which the continents only here and there emerge above the surface of the all-encircling sea.

Our remote forebears left the sea millions of years ago, but human blood is still much like sea water.

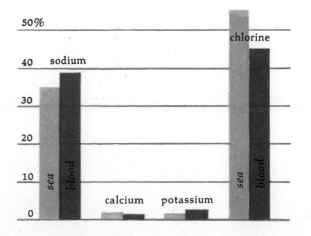

The Surface of the Sea

NOWHERE in all the sea is there so much life as in the surface waters.

From the deck of a vessel you may look down, hour after hour, on the shimmering discs of jellyfish, dotting the surface as far as you can see. Or you may notice early in the morning that you are passing through a sea that has taken on a brick-red color from billions upon billions of microscopic creatures, each of which contains a granule of orange coloring matter. At noon you are still moving through red seas. And when darkness falls, the waters shine with an eerie glow from the phosphorescent fires of yet more billions and trillions of these same creatures.

And again, as you look over the rail and down, down into water of a clear, deep green, suddenly there passes a silver shower of fishlets. The sun strikes a metallic gleam from their flanks as they streak by with the desperate speed of the hunted. Perhaps you never see the hunters. But you know they are there, for you see the gulls hovering, with eager, mewing cries, waiting for the little fish to be driven to the surface.

Or again, perhaps, you may sail for days on end and not see anything you recognize as life. Then you might say, "There is no spot on earth so empty of life as the open ocean!" But you would be wrong. If you were to tow a fine-meshed net through the seemingly lifeless water and then examine the washings of the net with a microscope, you would find that life is scattered almost everywhere through the surface waters like a fine dust. A cupful of water may contain millions upon millions of tiny plant cells, each of them far too small to be seen by the human eye. Or it may swarm with animal creatures, none larger than a

The surface of the sea has many colors and moods. The sullen, gray bleakness shown here is characteristic of the wind-lashed waters in southern latitudes known to sailors as the "Roaring Forties."

dust mote, which live on plant cells still smaller than themselves.

All this you might notice in the daytime, but if you could be close to the surface of the ocean at night, you would find that then it is alive with strange creatures never seen by day. This is because many sea animals can exist only in darkness or where the light is dim. After sunset some of them come up to the surface and swim about all night. But before dawn they must drop down again into deeper waters where the sun's rays cannot follow them.

The animals that must avoid sunlight are mostly small, shrimplike creatures, but they are followed to the surface by larger, hungry animals that try to capture them as food. When in 1947 the Norwegian scientist Thor Heyerdahl and his companions drifted across the Pacific on a raft, they were astonished by the change that took place in the surface life at night. Often they heard schools of small squids leaping out of the water in pursuit of prey. Twice a strange, deep-sea fish known as a snake mackerel jumped onto the raft. No one had ever seen this kind of fish before, except as a skeleton washed ashore on some beach.

For creatures of the sea, even those that live deep down and never come to the top, the surface waters are the most important part of the ocean. For it is there that the tiny plants live—the plants which directly or indirectly supply all the animals with food. These tiny vegetables—they are so small that you could not see an individual plant without a microscope—take the minerals of the sea and convert them into foodstuffs called carbohydrates. This is something no animal can do. Animals must eat plants to obtain the necessary minerals, or else they must eat other animals that have fed on plants.

Now, plants can live and carry on their work only where there is sunlight. For sea plants this means the upper 600 feet of water. So if for some reason the conditions at the surface of the sea are unfavorable and plants fail to grow and multiply there, there could also be a food shortage for a cod lying on a ledge of some rocky canyon far below— or for a bed of seaworms carpeting a shoal—or for a prawn creeping over the sea floor in blackness a mile down.

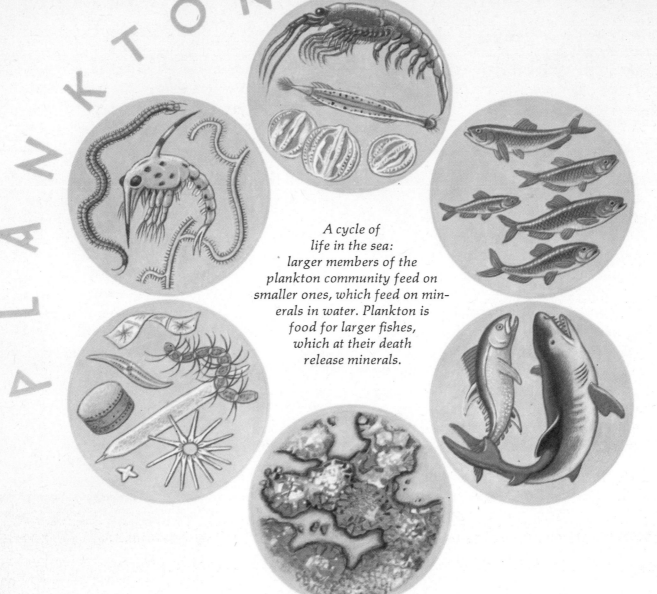

A cycle of life in the sea: larger members of the plankton community feed on smaller ones, which feed on minerals in water. Plankton is food for larger fishes, which at their death release minerals.

PLANKTON

The upper layers of the sea are inhabited by a strange community of plants and small animals. This community is called the plankton, from a Greek word that means "wandering." And, indeed, the drifting plankton does wander wherever the streaming currents of the sea carry it, for the living things that compose it have little if any power to swim.

Under a microscope a sample of plankton would seem very strange to us. Some creatures would appear as little transparent rods or chains. Some would look like thimbles or crescents or balls. We would see tiny, goblin-like creatures with huge eyes, glass-clear worms like fierce little dragons half an inch long, tiny, throbbing jellyfishes, and baby fishes of many different kinds.

Of the plants that inhabit the plankton, the diatoms are among the most abundant and most important as food for many different creatures. Each diatom is a single cell. You would see it under the microscope as a tiny box made of two pieces of glassy silica. Inside the box or shell is the living tissue of the plant. Some of the little balls and crescents in the plankton are one-celled animals that feed on diatoms. Many crustaceans, the young of crabs, barnacles, fishes, and other creatures do that, too. And other creatures of the plankton in turn feed on them. Enormous numbers of shrimp-like animals inhabit the plankton. Also the babies of a great variety of sea animals spend the first weeks of life as members of the plankton. The populations of these infant sea creatures change from week to week, for the parent animals have different seasons for spawning. At one time a plankton sample might contain billions of top-shaped larvae of the oyster. At another time it might swarm with odd little gnome-like creatures that are the larvae of some kind of crab.

The plankton is the basic foodstuff of the sea. Fishes like herring, mackerel, and menhaden feed on it, as do shellfish like oysters or clams. Large fish like bluefish, tuna, and sharks eat other fish that have fed on plankton. And the great whales, according to their kind, live on fishes or on shrimp or even on the smallest of the plankton creatures.

To us the surface of the ocean looks much the same from one shore to another. It seems not to be crossed by any tracks or marked by boundaries. But this is not really so. Although we cannot always see it, the ocean surface has a pattern—it is divided into definite zones made up of different kinds of water.

The zones we can make out most easily are those marked by color. The indigo blue of the open sea far from land tells us that this is an area containing little life. For the deep sea is blue because the water is very clear and sunlight can penetrate far into its depths. As light sinks into the sea, the colors that compose it are absorbed one by one, so that finally all the reds and yellows have been screened out and only the blues remain. It is this cool blue color that is reflected back to our eyes. On the other hand, green and sometimes even yellow and brown colors are common near land where rivers bring in quantities of minerals as a food supply. These colors tell us that plankton is abundant and therefore other life, too. Occasionally a tiny plant or animal form containing red pigment is so numerous in some locality that it causes the "red water" that has been known since ancient times in many parts of the world. The Red Sea takes its name from the fact that such red plankton often occurs there.

But the color of the sea is only an indirect sign of more important conditions that govern life in the sea. Parts of the sea are more salty than others. Some parts are warmer or colder than others. Both of these conditions affect living things directly.

This squid, which has fed on small fishes, will now be eaten by a bass.

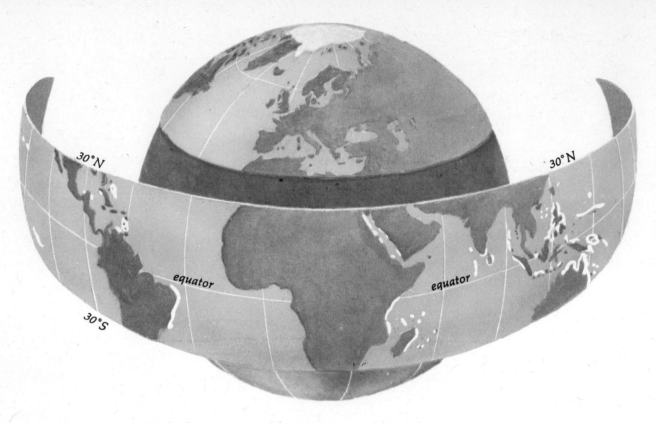

Corals, being extremely sensitive to cold, rarely grow outside a band that extends from 30° North to 30° South of the equator.

The saltiest ocean water in the world is that of the Red Sea. There the burning sun and the fierce heat of the atmosphere cause such rapid evaporation that the sea is 4 per cent salt. Of the oceans themselves, the Atlantic is the saltiest, and the saltiest part of the Atlantic is the Sargasso Sea. This sea, which is in an area of high temperatures, is so far from land that it gets no inflow of river water or melting ice. The polar seas, as one would expect, are the least salty, because they are constantly being diluted by rain, snow, and the melting of the ice.

As for temperature, it varies from about 28°F in polar seas to 96° in the Persian Gulf, which contains the hottest ocean water in the world. Now, most sea creatures have no way of keeping their body temperature at a constant level. Their temperature changes with that of the surrounding water. So the sea's temperature range of 68° is really of tremendous importance to its inhabitants. It has much to do with determining where a particular kind of animal may live.

The coral animals that build beautiful reefs of stonelike material are a good example. These animals are found only within a band extending from about 30° north latitude to about 30° south latitude within which the sea temperature is at least 70° Fahrenheit. The only corals that grow outside this band around the middle of the earth are found at Bermuda, at 32° north latitude, to which the Gulf Stream has carried water warm enough for the needs of the corals.

Temperature has a tremendous effect both on the kind and amount of marine life. So it is not surprising that there should be great differences between the sea life of the tropics and of polar seas. There is greater variety in the tropics—richly colored corals, mollusks with shells adorned with spines and turrets, fish with lacy fins and rainbow hues, worms with plumes like Oriental fans. This wonderful variety is possible because animals grow faster in warm water, and produce new generations in a shorter time. Nature has therefore had more chances to develop new forms. On the other hand, there are far fewer individuals of any one kind, compared with what we find in polar seas. In the tropics there are no such swarms of a single animal as there are of the copepods in the Arctic.

At first thought, the enormous abundance of life in icy seas is surprising. We would think the cold waters were inhospitable. But copepods and swimming snails fill the surface water of the cold seas and lure the herring and the mackerel, the flocks of sea birds, the whales, and the seals. Vast patches of a single kind of worm carpet the east coast of Spitsbergen. In the Barents Sea a research vessel once brought up more than a ton of one kind of sponge at a single haul.

This abundant life is possible because cold waters are richer in minerals than tropical seas. In warm waters there is little circulation or stirring of the water, and the minerals that pile up on the sea bottom tend to remain there. But in temperate and arctic regions the sea's temperature varies from season to season, and in the spring the cold surface water sinks and is replaced by warm water from below. This brings up quantities of minerals that nourish the plankton and all that feed on it.

Yet in the warm seas, too, there are places with a wealth of life. Here and there in tropical regions is a spot or band of water where the surface life is as abundant as on any arctic whaling ground. This happens where steeply rising currents bring up cold water from the deep sea—water carrying nourishing minerals. The Humboldt Current off the Pacific coast of South America is such a place. There the surface waters are teeming with plankton, fish, and sea birds.

It is in the middle of the oceans that life is scarce. These are the deserts of the sea. There are few birds and few surface-feeding fishes, and indeed there is little surface plankton to attract them. The life of these regions is largely down in the deep water. But the Sargasso Sea is an exception.

The Sargasso Sea is so different from any other place on earth that it may well be considered a definite geographic region. A line drawn from the mouth of the Chesapeake Bay to Gibraltar would skirt its northern border; another from Haiti to Dakar would mark its southern boundary. It lies all about Bermuda and extends more than half-way across the Atlantic. Roughly its area is as large as the United States. The Sargasso is a creation of the great currents of the North Atlantic that en-

In the enchantment of warm, sunlit seas, corals of many kinds live side by side, growing upward toward the light from the surface.

Some eight species of sargassum (one of them shown here) can be found adrift in the Sargasso Sea.

circle it and bring into it the millions of tons of floating sargassum weed, from which the place takes its name.

The Sargasso is a place forgotten by the winds. Under the seldom-clouded skies, its waters grow warm and heavy with salt. There is no fresh water coming in to dilute its saltiness, for it is far from coastal rivers and from polar ice. The only inflow is of salty water from the nearby currents, especially from the Gulf Stream. And with the little, inflowing streams come the plants and animals that for months or years have drifted in the Gulf Stream.

The sargassum weed is a brown sea weed that lives attached to rocks along the coasts of the West Indies and Florida. Storms tear away many of the plants, especially during the hurricane season. They are picked up by the Gulf Stream and are drifted northward. And with the weeds go, as accidental passengers, many small fishes, crabs, shrimps, and countless larvae of assorted marine creatures.

Curious things happen to the animals that have ridden on the sargassum weed into a new home. Once they lived on a rocky shore, a few feet or a

ATLANTIC

UNITED STATES

Bermudas

EUROPE

CUBA

Azores

SARGASSO SEA

HISPANIOLA

Madeira

Canary
Islands

OCEAN

SOUTH

AFRICA

AMERICA

few fathoms below the surface, but never far above a rocky bottom. They knew the rhythmic movements of waves and tides. They could leave the shelter of the sargassum weeds at will and creep or swim about over the bottom in search of food. Now, in the middle of the ocean, they are in a new world. The bottom lies two or three miles below them. Those who are poor swimmers must cling to the weed, which now represents a life raft, supporting them above the deep sea. Over the ages since their ancestors came here, some species have developed special organs of attachment either for themselves or for their eggs, so that they may not sink into the cold, dark water far below.

Many of the little marine beasts of the weedy jungle seem to be playing an elaborate game of disguise. Each is camouflaged to hide it from the others. The Sargasso sea slug—a snail without a shell—has a soft, shapeless brown body spotted with dark-edged circles and fringed with flaps and folds of skin. As it creeps over the weed in search of prey, it can scarcely be distinguished from the vegetation. One of the fiercest flesh-eaters of the place, a fish, has copied in every detail the golden

27

berries of the sargassum, its branching fronds, its rich brown color. The fish is even marked with white dots that look exactly like the hard little worm tubes that often become attached to the sea weed. All these elaborate bits of imitation tell us that fierce wars go on in the Sargasso jungles, without mercy for the weak or the unwary.

But how did the Sargasso come by its drifting weeds?

There has been a long-standing argument about that. Some have held that the supply is kept up by weeds recently torn away from coastal beds. Others say this is impossible. They say the sargassum fields of the West Indies and Florida are too limited to supply the immense sea of the Sargasso. Here, they say, is a community of plants that maintains itself. The plants have become adapted to life in the open sea, need no roots or holdfasts for attachment, and are able to propagate by breaking off bits to grow into new plants. Probably there is truth in both ideas.

New plants do come in each year in small numbers. It takes about half a year for the plants torn from West Indian shores to reach the northern border of the Sargasso, perhaps several years for them to be carried into the inner parts of this area.

Meanwhile some have been swept onto the shores of North America by storms, and others have been killed by cold. But the plants that reach the calm of the Sargasso seem to live forever. The individual plants may live, some for decades, some for centuries, according to their kind. It might well be that some of the very weeds you would see if you visited the place today were seen by Columbus and his men. Here in the heart of the Atlantic, the weed drifts endlessly, growing, propagating. Apparently almost the only plants that die are the ones that drift into unfavorable conditions around the edges of the Sargasso or are picked up by outward-moving currents.

Such losses are balanced, or even more than balanced, by the weeds that yearly come from distant coasts. It must have taken eons of time to gather the enormous quantities of weed, which are estimated to be about 10 million tons. But this, of course, is distributed over so large an area that most of the Sargasso is open water. The dense fields of weeds which sailors once believed were waiting to entrap a vessel never existed except in their imagination. The gloomy hulks of ships doomed to endless drifting in the clinging weed are only the ghosts of things that never were.

The sargassum fish looks so much like the weeds that surround it that it is hard to find. Grapelike floaters keep the weeds near the sunlight.

On distant beaches migrating terns alight to rear their young.

The Changing Year

FOR THE sea as a whole the change from day to night and from season to season has no meaning. Such changes are lost in the vastness of the ocean. But the surface waters are different. They are always changing. Sparkling in the sun, mysterious in the twilight, their moods change from hour to hour. The surface waters move with the tides. They stir to the breath of the winds. Most of all, they change with the advance of the seasons.

On land, a thousand signs tell us that spring is on the way. For spring comes to the temperate lands of our northern hemisphere in a surge of new life. Green shoots push forth, buds unfold, the birds migrate northward, a chorus of frogs rises from the wet lands. There is spring even in the different sound the wind makes as it stirs the young leaves. It is easy to suppose that at sea there can be no such feeling of advancing spring. But the signs are there, and to one who understands them, they bring the same magical sense of awakening.

In the sea, as on land, spring is a time for the renewal of life. Before life can come, however, food must be provided. Just as land plants depend on minerals in the soil for their growth, so every plant of the sea, even the smallest, depends upon the nourishing salts or minerals in the water. Rich stores of these minerals have been gathering on the floor of the continental shelf. Some have been carried down from the land. Some have come from sea creatures, large and small, plant and animal, that have drifted down to the bottom. The waters must be deeply stirred to bring these minerals up. During the long months of winter in the temperate zones the surface waters have been absorbing the cold. Now in spring the heavy water begins to sink, slipping down and taking the place of the warmer layers below. As the warm bottom water is pushed up, it brings the minerals with it.

29

day. The young of fishes and crabs and mussels and tube worms mingle for a time with the year-round members of the plankton.

Under the steady, hungry grazing, the grasslands are soon reduced. The diatoms become more and more scarce and with them the other simple plants. Still there are brief outbursts of one or another of them. So, for a time each spring, the waters may become blotched with jellylike masses of a simple brown seaweed. Then the fishermen's nets come up dripping a brown slime and containing no fish. For the herring have turned away from these waters as though driven out by the foul-smelling algae. But in less than two weeks the waters have cleared again.

In the spring the sea is filled with migrating fishes. Some of them are bound for the mouths of great rivers, which they will ascend to lay their eggs. Such are the spring-run chinook salmon coming in from the deep Pacific feeding grounds to the Columbia. Such are the shad moving in to the Chesapeake and the Hudson and the Connecticut. The alewives or river herring seek a hundred coastal streams of New England; the Atlantic salmon feel their way to the Penobscot and the Kennebec. For months or years these fish have known only the vast spaces of the ocean. Now the spring sea and the maturing of their own bodies lead them back to the rivers of their birth.

As the season advances, other mysterious com-

A summer swarm of Noctiluca colors Atlantic waters.

Some of these chemicals have been in short supply in winter, and the diatom population has had to tide itself over as best it could. It has kept alive the spark of life by forming tough protective spores. In this state the diatoms have held their place in the winter sea, like seeds of wheat in a field under snow and ice—the seeds from which the spring growth will now come.

In the warmth of the spring sun there is a sudden awakening—the simplest plants of the sea begin to multiply. They increase with unbelievable speed. The spring sea belongs at first to the diatoms and to all the other tiny vegetables of the plankton. They cover vast areas of ocean with a living blanket of their cells. Mile after mile of water may appear red or brown or green, the whole surface taking on the color of the tiny grains of coloring matter in each of the plant cells.

But plants rule the sea for only a short time. Almost at once the small animals of the plankton begin to rival them in numbers. It is the spawning time of the copepod and the glassworm, the ocean shrimp and the winged snail. Now in the spring the surface waters become a vast nursery. From the continent's edge lying far below, and from the scattered shoals and banks, the eggs or young of many of the bottom animals drift up to the surface of the sea. Even those which later on will sink to a settled life on the bottom spend their first weeks as freely swimming hunters of the plankton. New batches of larvae rise into the surface each

Night falls, and like millions of stars these Noctiluca fill the waters with light.

ings and goings take place. Fish called capelin gather north of Russia in the deep, cold water of the Barents Sea. Flocks of birds such as auks, fulmars, and kittiwakes follow and prey upon their shoals. Cod gather off the shores of Norway and Iceland. Birds which in winter fed over the whole Atlantic, or the whole Pacific, make for some small island. The entire breeding population arrives there within the space of a few days. Whales suddenly appear off the coastal banks where the shrimplike krill are spawning. But where the whales came from or by what route no one knows.

When most of the spawning is over, life in the surface waters slackens to the slower pace of midsummer. Now the pale moon jelly Aurelia gathers in thousands where the currents meet. There it forms winding lines across the sea, and the birds see the creatures shimmering in the green water. By midsummer the large red jellyfish moves through the sea, trailing long tentacles. And as likely as not a little group of young cod or haddock find shelter under its bell and travel with it.

A brilliant phosphorescence often lights up the summer sea. In waters where the protozoan Noc-

tiluca abounds, it is the chief source of this summer light. Fishes, squids, or dolphins clothe themselves in the ghostly radiance. They fill the water with racing flame. Or again the summer sea may glitter with a thousand thousand moving pin pricks of light coming from a shoal of brilliantly phosphorescent shrimp.

Now, for the first time since spring, the dry twitter of the phalaropes is heard over the plankton meadows of the Atlantic. The small brown birds wheel and turn, dip and rise. The phalaropes have nested on the bare arctic plains. They have reared their young and now the first of them are returning to the sea. Most of them will continue south over the open water far from land. They will cross the equator into the South Atlantic. Here they will follow where the great whales lead, for where the whales are, there also are the swarms of plankton on which these strange little birds grow fat.

As the fall approaches, there are other movements that are signs of the end of summer. In the foggy waters of Bering Sea, to the north of the Aleutian Islands, the herds of fur seals are moving southward into the open Pacific. They have left

31

behind two small treeless islands. The islands are silent now, but for several months of summer they resounded with the roar of millions of seals come ashore to bear and rear their young. All the fur seals of the eastern Pacific crowded into those few square miles of bare volcanic rock and crumbling soil—the Pribilof Islands. Now once more the seals turn south, to roam down along the continent's edge, where it falls away steeply into the deep sea. Here, in total darkness, the seals will find rich feeding as they swim down to prey on the fishes.

Autumn comes to the sea with a fresh blaze of phosphorescence. Now every wave crest is aflame. Here and there the whole surface may glow with sheets of cold fire, while below, schools of fish pour through the water like molten metal. Often the phosphorescence is caused by the dinoflagellates, tiny plants which have multiplied furiously in fall as they did in the spring. Seen from the deck of a vessel at sea, it has an eerie, unearthly, disturbing quality. Man is given to thinking that any light not of moon or stars or sun has a human origin. Lights on shore, lights moving over the water, mean lights kindled and controlled by other men. But here are lights that flash and fade away, lights that come and go for reasons he cannot understand.

On such a night of phosphorescent display Charles Darwin stood on the deck of the *Beagle* as she plowed southward through the Atlantic off the coast of Brazil.

The sea from its extreme luminousness presented a wonderful and most beautiful appearance (he wrote in his diary). *Every part of the water which by day is seen as foam, glowed with a pale light. The vessel drove before her bows two billows of liquid phosphorus, and in her wake was a milky train. As far as the eye reached, the crest of every wave was bright; and from the reflected light, the sky just above the horizon was not so utterly dark as the rest of the Heavens. It was impossible to behold this plain of matter, as it were melted and consumed by heat, without being reminded of Milton's description of the regions of Chaos and Anarchy.*

Like the blazing colors of the autumn leaves before they wither and fall, the autumn phosphorescence hints that winter is approaching. Now the flagellates and the tiny algae dwindle away to a scattered few. So do the shrimps and the copepods, the glassworms and the comb jellies. The larvae that in spring rose from the bottom have long since grown up and drifted away to take up whatever existence is their lot. Even the roving fish schools have gone from the surface waters. They have migrated into warmer latitudes or have found equal warmth in the deep, quiet waters along the edge of the continental shelf.

The surface waters now become the plaything of the winter gales. The winds build up the giant storm waves and roar along their crests, lashing the water into foam and flying spray. It seems as if life must have deserted this place forever.

But this is not true. Hopeful signs are to be found even in the grayness and bleakness of the winter sea.

that before many weeks it must become so heavy that it will plunge downward and start the overturn that is the first act in the drama of spring. There is promise of new life in the small plantlike things that cling to the rocks of the underlying bottom. From these polyps a new generation of jellyfish will bud off and rise into the surface waters. There is promise in the sluggish forms of the copepods lying on the bottom. They are not dead. Safe from the surface storms, they are hibernating, kept alive by the extra store of fat with which they went into their winter sleep.

Already, from the cod that have moved through the cold sea to their spawning places, eggs are rising into the surface waters. Even in the harsh world of the winter sea, these glassy eggs will begin to develop into living fishlets.

Most of all, perhaps, there is promise in the fine dust of life that remains in the surface waters. The invisible spores of the diatoms need only the touch of warming sun and fertilizing chemicals to repeat the magic of spring.

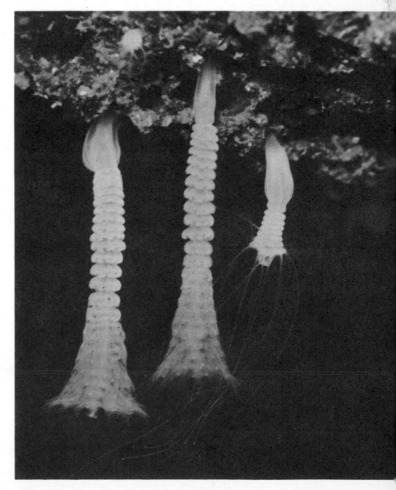

On land we know that winter, though it appears lifeless, is not really so. Look closely at the bare branches of a tree on which not the palest gleam of green can be seen. Spaced along each branch are the leaf buds. Concealed and safely preserved under the overlapping layers is all the spring's magic of swelling green. Pick off a piece of the rough bark of the trunk. There you will find hibernating insects. Dig down through the snow into the earth. There are the dormant seeds from which will come the grass, the herb, the oak tree.

So, too, the lifelessness of the winter sea is only seeming. Everywhere are the promises that spring will come again.

There is promise of it in the very iciness of the winter sea, in the chilling of the water. We know

These curious creatures clinging to the rock will one day become several dozen animals of a very different kind. As the waters become warmer, the end rings will, one by one, bud off and become jellyfishes.

33

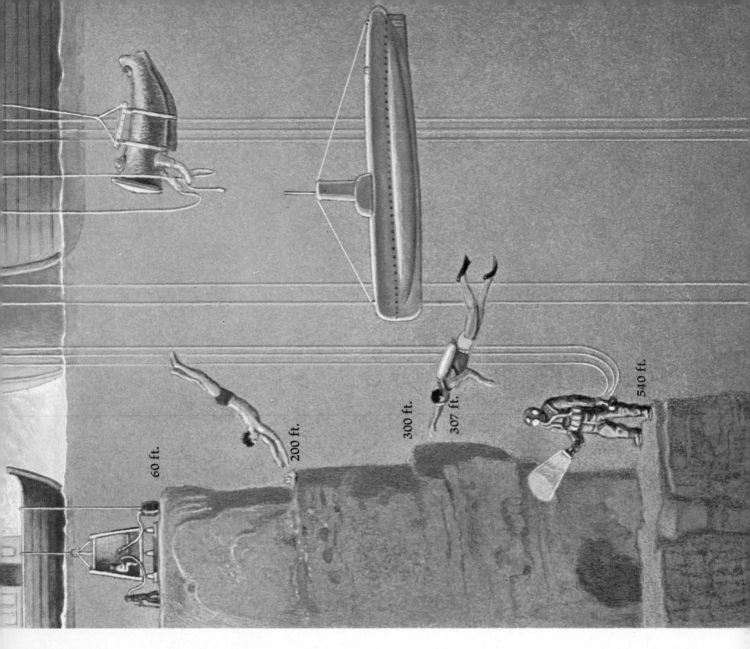

60 ft.

200 ft.

300 ft.

307 ft.

540 ft.

The Sunless Sea

BETWEEN the sunlit surface and the hidden ocean floor lies the least known region of the sea. These deep, dark waters, with all their mysteries, cover a very large part of the earth. The whole world ocean extends over about three-fourths of the globe. If we subtract the shallow areas, where at least the pale ghost of sunlight moves over the bottom, there still remains about half the earth that is covered by miles-deep water that has been dark since the world began.

Man has so far been able to venture only to the threshold of this region. Carrying tanks of compressed air, he can swim down to depths of about 300 feet. With the gas helium, instead of air, he can go somewhat deeper. He can descend to about 500 feet wearing a diving helmet and a rubberized suit. Only a few men in all the history of the world have gone down alive beyond the range of visible light. The first to do so were William Beebe and Otis Barton. In the bathysphere, they reached a depth of 3028 feet in the open ocean off Bermuda, in the year 1934. Barton alone, in a steel sphere of somewhat different design, descended to 4500 feet off California, in the summer of 1949. In 1954 French divers reached the great depth of two and a half miles off the coast of Africa. So each record set is soon broken. Some day man's engineering skill may carry daring explorers to the deepest part of the sea.

3028 ft.

4500 ft.

13,287 ft.

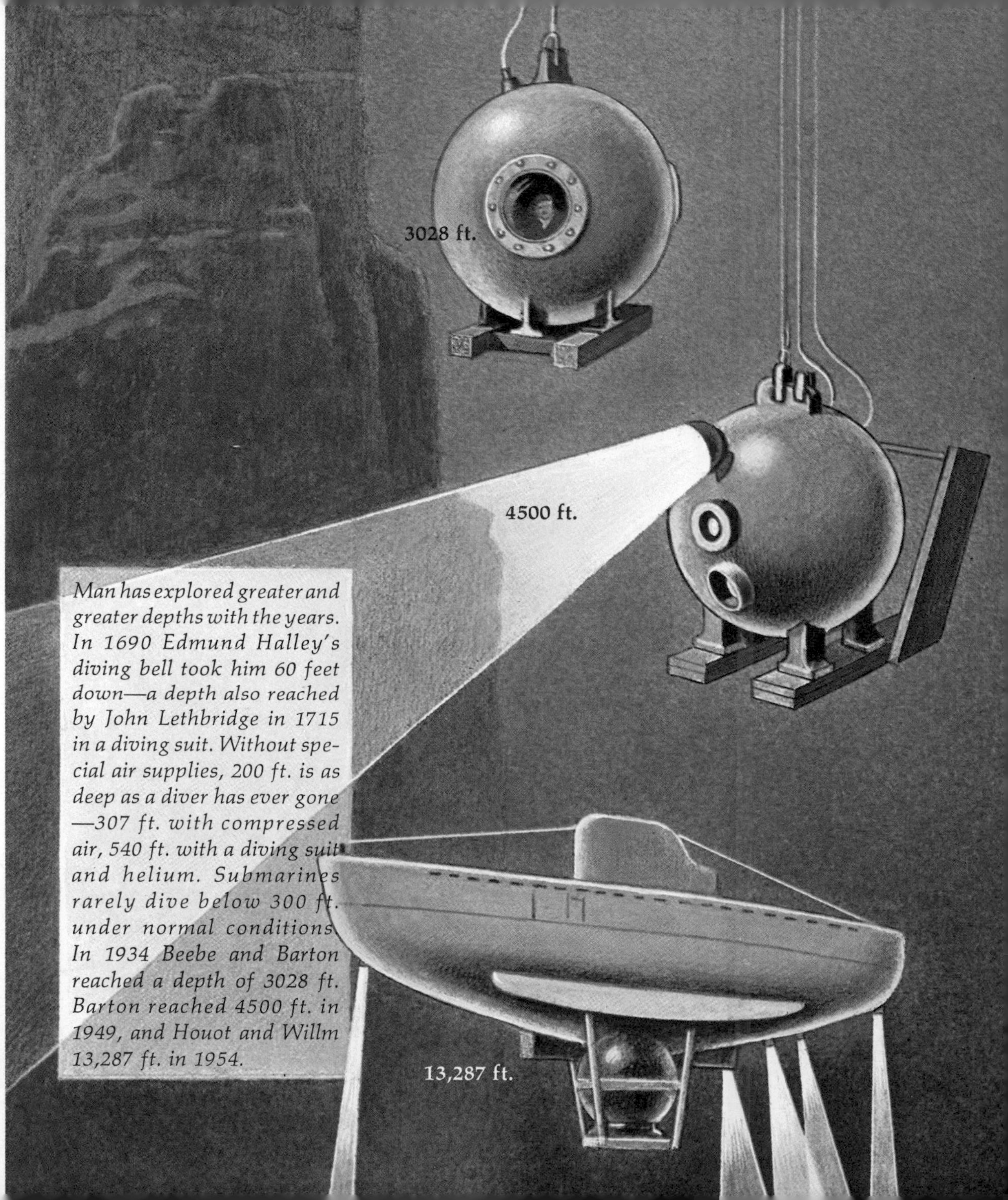

Man has explored greater and greater depths with the years. In 1690 Edmund Halley's diving bell took him 60 feet down—a depth also reached by John Lethbridge in 1715 in a diving suit. Without special air supplies, 200 ft. is as deep as a diver has ever gone —307 ft. with a diving suit, 540 ft. with a diving suit and helium. Submarines rarely dive below 300 ft. under normal conditions. In 1934 Beebe and Barton reached a depth of 3028 ft. Barton reached 4500 ft. in 1949, and Houot and Willm 13,287 ft. in 1954.

But although only a fortunate few can ever visit the deep sea, the instruments of the oceanographer —which record pressure, saltiness, temperature, and light penetration—have enabled us to reconstruct in imagination these eerie, forbidding regions. The deep waters are a place of unending night, as old as the sea itself. For most of its creatures, groping their way endlessly through its black water, it must be a place of hunger, where food is scarce and hard to find, a shelterless place where there is no refuge from ever-present enemies. It is a place where one can only move on and on, from birth to death, through an endless night, confined as in a prison to his own particular layer of the sea.

They used to say that nothing could live in the deep sea. It was a belief that must have been easy to accept. For without proof to the contrary, how could anyone conceive of life in such a place?

Yet even as far back as 1818 proof was found. In that year, Sir John Ross, exploring the arctic seas, brought up from a depth of 1000 fathoms— 6000 feet—mud in which there were worms. So there *was* animal life in the bed of the deep ocean! It existed in spite of the darkness and the immense pressure of more than a mile of water above.

Then in 1860 came another report. The surveying ship *Bulldog* was examining a route for a cable from Faroe to Labrador. The *Bulldog's* sounding line, which at one place had been allowed to lie for some time on the bottom at a depth of 1260 fathoms, came up with 13 starfish clinging to it. The deep had sent forth the long-desired message! But not all the scientists of the day were prepared

35

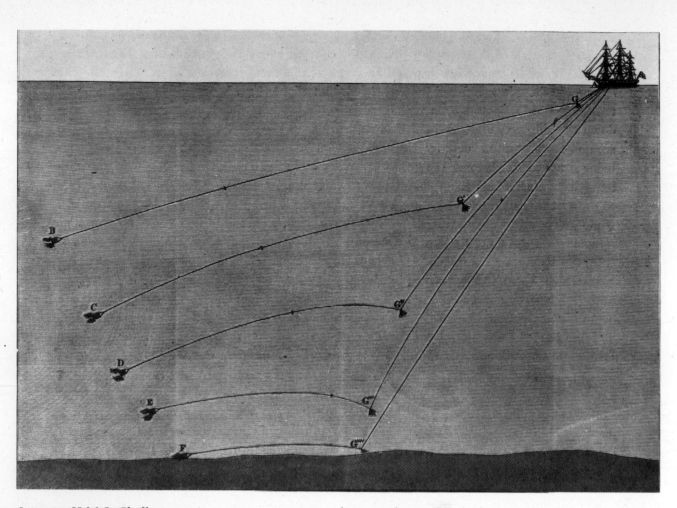

In 1872, H.M.S. Challenger *set out on an oceanographic expedition, in which it circled the world in three and a half years. Here we see the* Challenger *raking the water with its samplers, each weighted with a sinker.*

to accept it. Some declared that the starfish had "convulsively embraced" the line somewhere on the way back to the surface.

Further evidence was on the way, however. In that same year a cable in the Mediterranean was raised for repairs from a depth of 1200 fathoms, and it was found to be heavily encrusted with corals and other animals that had clearly been living and growing on the cable for months or years. There was not the slightest chance that they had become entangled in it as it was being raised to the surface.

A dozen years later all doubts about life in the great depths came to an end. The *Challenger*, the first ship ever equipped for oceanographic exploration, set out from England in the year 1872 and traced a course around the globe. From bottoms lying under miles of water and from all the light-less depths above, net-haul after net-haul of strange and fantastic creatures came up and were spilled out on the decks. Poring over the weird beings thus brought up for the first time into the light of day, beings no man had ever seen before, the *Challenger* scientists realized that life existed even on the deepest floor of the abyss.

One of the most exciting things ever learned about the ocean was discovered only recently. It is the fact that a living cloud of some unknown creatures is spread over much of the ocean at a depth of several hundred fathoms below the surface.

This information came to us in a curious manner. New instruments had been designed to let ships under way record the depths of the ocean. Sound waves were directed downward like a beam of light and an echo came back from the bottom. Probably no one suspected that these instruments would be a means of learning something about

*Nets and collection bottles, attached to hemp lines,
hang amid the intricate rigging of the* Challenger.

deep-sea life. But operators soon discovered that
the sound waves were reflected back from any
solid object they met on the way. Answering
echoes came first from something part way down,
and then a second echo was received from the
bottom. Presumably the first echoes came from
schools of fish, whales, or submarines.

These facts were well established by the 1930's.
Then in 1946 the United States Navy reported
that several scientists, working with echo-sounding
equipment in deep water off the California coast,
had discovered a widespread "layer" of some sort,
which gave back an answering echo to the sound
waves. This reflecting layer seemed to be sus-
pended between the surface and the floor of the
Pacific and was found over an area 300 miles wide.
It lay from 1000 to 1500 feet below the surface.

But what was this layer?

In this shipboard laboratory (below) Challenger *scientists examined their catch.*

Chinese visitors, an elephant, a giraffe, and a few Osage Indians all help give an idea of the huge size of a blue whale—the largest of all animals.

The first clue was given by Martin W. Johnson of the Scripps Institution of Oceanography, who had been working aboard the *E. W. Scripps*— part of this vessel can be seen in the photograph at the top of page 56. He found that whatever it was that sent back the echoes moved upward and downward in rhythmic fashion. It was up near the surface at night, down in deep water during the day. Clearly the layer must be made up of living creatures who could move at will.

From this time on, discoveries about the sea's "phantom bottom" came rapidly. The living layer is not something peculiar to the coast of California alone. It occurs almost everywhere in deep ocean basins. Across the Pacific it seems to exist almost unbroken. By day the layer drifts at a depth of several hundred fathoms, at night it rises to the surface, and again, before sunrise, it sinks into the depths. Whatever makes up the layer is apparently strongly repelled by sunlight. But what is the power that repels? And what attraction draws the creatures toward the surface? Is it comparative safety from enemies that makes them seek dark-

ness? Is it more abundant food near the surface that lures them back under cover of night?

Attempts to sample the layer and to photograph it have been made. Yet no one is sure of what creatures it is composed.

But what do the eye-witness accounts tell us of life in these mid-depths?

They, too, speak of abundant life. William Beebe was not prepared for what he saw from the bathysphere. Although over a period of six years he had made many hundreds of net-hauls in the same area, he was amazed by the abundance and variety of life that surrounded him in the depths. More than a quarter of a mile down, he reported collections of living things as thick "as I have ever seen them." At half a mile—which is as far down as he went—Dr. Beebe recalled that "there was no instant when a mist of plankton . . . was not swirling in the path of the beam."

Professor Auguste Piccard and his son, Jacques, who made many deep dives during the early 1950's, report that they seldom saw large fishes. There were many smaller creatures—jellyfishes, crabs,

38

The sperm whale, or cachalot, is the largest of the toothed whales. Unlike blue whales, which feed on plankton, sperm whales prey mainly on squids and octopuses, of which they can eat up to a ton a day.

starfishes, and plankton. On the deep sea bottoms they visited they saw many holes from which the heads of small fishes looked out. The fish seemed not to notice the bright lights turned toward them by the human visitors to their world, although sometimes they swam away at great speed.

Man is not the first to find out that there is abundant life in the deep sea. Probably millions of years ago certain whales made the discovery. The ancestors of all whales, we know, were land mammals. They must have been beasts that preyed on other animals, if we are to judge by their powerful jaws and teeth. Perhaps in searching for food about the deltas of great rivers or around the edges of shallow seas, they discovered the wealth of fish and other marine life. Over the centuries they formed the habit of following them farther and farther into the sea, and little by little their bodies took on a form more suitable for life in the water. Their hind limbs were reduced so that only dissection can show us the tiny stubs that are all that remain. The forelimbs were changed into organs for steering and balancing.

Eventually the whales, as though to divide the sea's food among them, became separated into three groups: the plankton-eaters, the fish-eaters, and the squid-eaters. The plankton-eating whales can exist only where there are dense masses of small shrimp or copepods for them to feed upon.

This limits them almost entirely to arctic and ant-arctic waters and the high temperate latitudes. Fish-eating whales may find food over a somewhat wider range of ocean. But they must stay in places where there are enormous populations of schooling fish. The blue water of the tropics and of the open ocean basins offers little to either of these groups. The sperm whale has a far wider range. For this immense, square-headed, toothed whale discovered long ago what men have known for only a short time—that hundreds of fathoms below the almost uninhabited surface waters of the blue ocean there is a wealth of animal life.

The sperm whale has taken these deep waters for his hunting grounds. His quarry is the deep-water population of squids, including the giant squid, which lives at depths of 1500 feet or more. The head of the sperm whale is often marked with long stripes, which consist of a great number of circular scars made by the suckers of the squid. Seeing these scars, we are led to picture in our imagination the unseen combats that must go on in the darkness of the deep water between these two huge creatures. Imagine the sperm whale with its 70-ton bulk battling the squid with a body as long as 30 feet, and writhing, grasping arms that bring the total length of the animal to perhaps 50 feet!

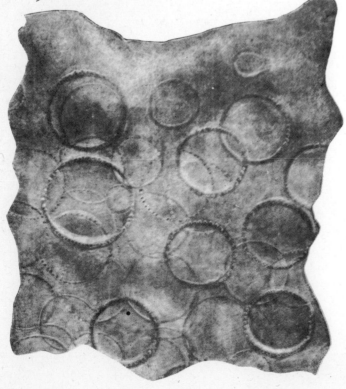

The sperm whale and the giant squid are deadly enemies. There may be one less squid in the sea after the battle, but the head of the whale will be forever scarred. A close view of such scars is shown at left.

The greatest depth at which the giant squid lives is not definitely known. But we do know something about the depth to which sperm whales descend, presumably in search of the squids. In April 1932 the cable repair ship *All America* was investigating what seemed to be a break in a submarine cable. It was brought to the surface off the shore of Colombia, on the Pacific coast of South America. Entangled in it was a dead 45-foot sperm whale. The submarine cable was twisted around the lower jaw and was wrapped around one flipper, the body, and the tail. The cable had been raised from a depth of 3240 feet, almost two-thirds of a mile.

Some of the seals also appear to have discovered the hidden food reserves of the deep ocean. It has long been something of a mystery where, and on what, the northern fur seals of the eastern Pacific feed during the winter, which they spend off the coast of North America from California to Alaska. There is no evidence that they are feeding to any great extent on sardines, mackerel, or other fishes important to commerce. For four million seals could hardly compete with commercial fishermen for the same fishes without the fact being known.

But there is some evidence on what the fur seals eat. And this food gives us a hint about the depths at which they feed. In the stomachs of seals have been found the bones of a kind of fish that has never been seen alive. Indeed, not even its remains have been found anywhere else. Fish experts say that this "seal fish" belongs to a group that inhabits very deep water, off the edge of the continental shelf.

There is one puzzling question about this deep-sea feeding of whales and seals. They are warm-blooded mammals like ourselves. How do they stand the tremendous pressure changes when they dive several hundred fathoms? Human divers die if rapidly brought up from depths of 200 feet or so. They are killed by caisson disease, which is caused by the rapid collecting of nitrogen bubbles in the blood when pressure is suddenly released. Yet whalers say a balleen whale, when harpooned, can dive straight down to a depth of half a mile—as measured by the amount of line carried out. From these depths, where pressure on every inch of its body is half a ton, it returns almost immediately to the surface. What the answer is we really do not know. The most reasonable explanation is this. The diver has air pumped to him while he is under water. The whale, on the other hand, has only the limited supply it carried down and does not have enough nitrogen in its blood to do serious harm.

Young killer whale beached near Cape Hatteras.

You might wonder how it is that creatures so fragile as the glass sponge and the jellyfish can endure the immense pressure of deep water. At first thought it does seem amazing. But the answer is that for creatures at home in the deep sea the pressure inside their tissues is the same as that outside. As long as this balance is preserved, there is no problem. They are no more inconvenienced by a pressure of a ton or so than we are by ordinary atmospheric pressure. And most creatures of the deep, it must be remembered, never have to adjust themselves to extreme changes of pressure.

Of course, there are exceptions. And they are the real miracle, not the animal that lives its whole life on the bottom, bearing a pressure of perhaps five or six tons. The really amazing creatures are those that regularly move up and down through hundreds or thousands of feet of change. The small shrimps and other planktonic creatures that go down into deep water during the day are examples, and how they do it with safety we do not know.

Change of pressure does, however, make a serious problem for fishes that have air bladders. Anyone who has seen a trawler's net raised from a hundred fathoms knows this and realizes that such fish must be wary of more than the net. They must be careful to stay in their own zone, to which they are adjusted. For if, while pursuing their food, fish wander upward beyond the invisible boundary of their zone, they may not be able to return. The pressure up there being less, it causes the gas in the air bladder to expand. The fish becomes lighter and more buoyant. Perhaps he tries to fight his way down again, opposing the upward lift with all the power of his muscles. If he does not succeed, he "falls" to the surface, injured and dying. For the sudden release of pressure from outside causes the tissues to stretch and burst.

The compression of the sea under its own weight is relatively slight, and there is no basis for the old and picturesque belief that, at the deeper levels, the water resists the downward passage of objects from the surface. According to this belief, sinking ships, the bodies of drowned men, and presumably the bodies of the larger sea animals not consumed by hungry scavengers, never reach the bottom, but come to rest at some level determined by the relation of their own weight to the compression of the

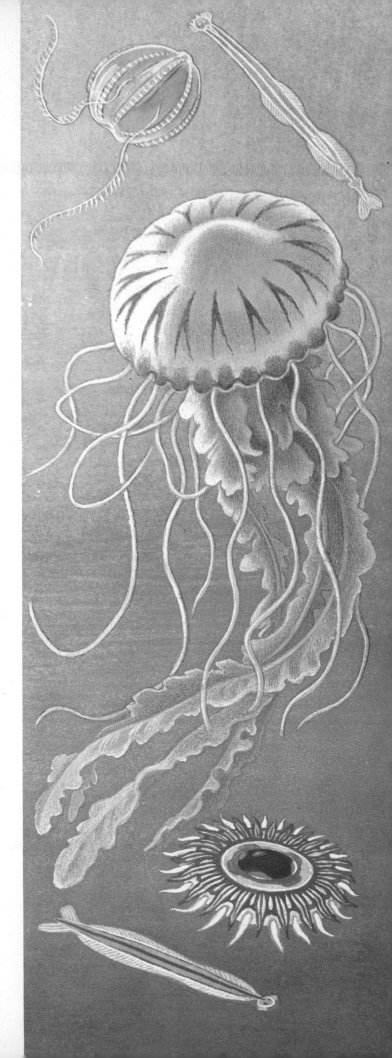

A chrysaora jellyfish sweeps by, trailing its long tentacles in the Atlantic waters. Above it are two nearly transparent creatures of surface waters, a little comb jelly (left) and an arrowworm. Below it are a darker arrowworm and jellyfish of deeper waters.

water, there to drift forever. The fact is that anything will continue to sink as long as its specific gravity is greater than that of the surrounding water, and all large bodies descend, in a matter of a few days, to the ocean floor. As mute testimony to this fact, we bring up from the deepest ocean basins the teeth of sharks and the hard ear bones of whales.

Immense pressure, then, is one of the ruling conditions in the deep sea. Darkness is another. The unchanging darkness of the deep waters has done weird and unbelievable things to the animals that inhabit them.

For one thing it has affected their color. In a curious way, the colors of marine animals tend to be related to the zone in which they live. Fishes of the surface waters, like the mackerel and herring, often are blue or green. So are the floats of the Portuguese men-of-war and the azure-tinted wings of the swimming snails. Lower down—below the diatom meadows and the drifting sargassum weed—where the water becomes ever more deeply and brilliantly blue, many creatures are crystal clear. Their glassy, ghostly forms blend with their surroundings and make it easier for them to escape the ever-present, ever-hungry enemy. Such are the transparent hordes of the arrowworms or glassworms, the comb jellies, and the larvae of many different kinds of fishes.

At a thousand feet, and on down to the very end of the sun's rays, silvery fishes are common, and many others are red, drab brown, or black. Pteropods are a dark violet. Arrowworms, whose relatives in the upper layers are colorless, are here a deep red. Jellyfish, which above would be transparent, are a deep brown at a depth of 1000 feet.

At depths greater than 1500 feet, all the fishes are black, deep violet, or brown. But the shrimps wear amazing hues of red, scarlet, and purple. Why, no one can say, for in the darkness of the bottom they can only look black to their neighbors.

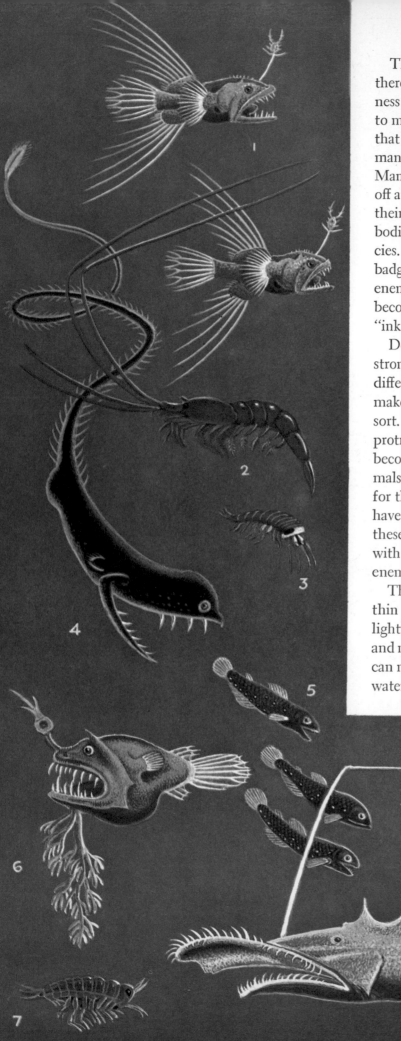

The deep sea has its stars, and perhaps here and there an eerie temporary moonlight. For the darkness of the lower depths has forced many creatures to make their own light. Perhaps half of the fishes that live in dimly lit or darkened water, as well as many of the lower forms, are phosphorescent. Many fishes carry torches that can be turned on or off at will, presumably to help them find or pursue their prey. Others have rows of lights over their bodies, in patterns that vary from species to species. This may be a sort of recognition mark or badge by which the fish can be known as friend or enemy. The deep-sea squid spurts out a fluid that becomes a cloud of light—the duplicate of the "ink" of his shallow-water relative.

Down beyond the reach of even the longest and strongest of the sun's rays, the eyes of fishes are different. They become enlarged, as though to make the most of any chance light of whatever sort. Or they may be telescopic, large of lens, and protruding. Some fishes, on the other hand, have become blind, as has happened to certain cave animals that live in a world of darkness. To make up for their lack of eyes, the blind animals of the sea have marvelous feelers and long, slender fins. With these they grope their way like so many blind men with canes. They get their whole knowledge of enemies or food through the sense of touch.

The last traces of plants are left behind in the thin upper layer of water. Few find enough sunlight for the manufacture of food below 200 feet, and none lives below 600 feet. And since no animal can make its own food, the creatures of the deeper waters live a strange life, utterly dependent on the upper layers. These hungry flesh-eaters prey fiercely upon each other, yet the whole community depends in the end upon the slow rain of food particles descending from above.

This never-ending rain is made up of the dead and dying plants and animals from the surface, or from one of the layers in between. It is a strange rain—the lower it goes the less there is of it. For each of the populations that lie between the surface and the sea bottom snaps up what it can as the rain passes through. In general the food supply is poorer from tier to tier, and down in the lowest layer of living beings the competition for food is very fierce indeed. Some hint of its fierceness is seen in the saber-toothed jaws of some of the small, dragonlike fishes of the deeper waters, in the immense mouths, and in the elastic bodies that make it possible for a fish to swallow another several times its size.

Pressure and darkness are the conditions of life in the deep sea. Only a few years ago we should have added silence, but we know now that the notion of the sea as a silent place is wholly false. Wide experience with hydrophones and other listening devices for detecting submarines has upset that idea. Around the shore lines of much of the world there is an extraordinary uproar made by fishes, shrimps, porpoises, and probably other forms not yet recognized. There has been little investigation as yet of sound in the deep, offshore areas. However, when the crew of the research vessel *Atlantis* lowered a hydrophone into deep water off Bermuda, they recorded strange mewing sounds, shrieks, and ghostly moans. We do not

yet know by what creatures these sounds are made. But fish of shallower zones have been captured and put into aquaria, where their voices have been recorded for comparison with sounds at sea.

One of the most extraordinarily widespread sounds of the undersea is the crackling, sizzling noise, like dry twigs burning or fat frying, heard near beds of the snapping shrimp. This is a small, round shrimp, about an inch across, with one very large claw which it uses to stun its prey. The claw bears a movable finger that is raised and then snapped back into position with a loud click. At the same time a jet of water spurts out. This activity, carried on by thousands of shrimps, produces the noise called shrimp crackle. No one had any idea the little snapping shrimps were so abundant or so widely distributed until their signals began to be picked up on hydrophones.

Sometimes the noise made by sea animals creates difficult problems for man. During the Second World War a hydrophone network was set up by the United States Navy to protect the entrance to Chesapeake Bay. In the spring of 1942 the speakers at the surface suddenly began to give

On these pages are some of the inhabitants of the cold, dark regions of the deep sea: 1 Caulophryne acinosa, 2 Sergestes robustus, 3 Scypholanceola, 4 Saccopharynx johnsoni, 5 Lampanyctus, 6 Linophryne arborifer, 7 Lanceola, 8 Lasiognathus, 9 Sternoptyx, 10 Argyropelecus, 11 Melanocetus cirrifer, 12 Chauliodus sloanei, 13 Nemichthys.

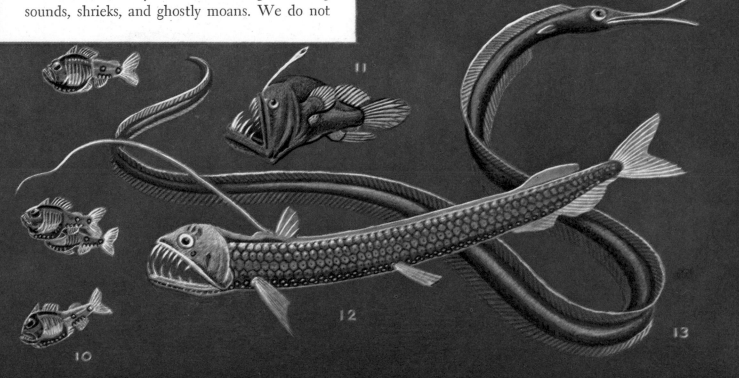

An underwater microphone will detect the sounds made by the parrotfish as it grinds up bits of coral.

forth every evening a sound like "a pneumatic drill tearing up pavement." The network was useless. What were these strange noises that completely masked the sounds of passing ships? Finally the mystery was solved. The sounds were the voices of fish known as croakers, which in the spring move into Chesapeake Bay from their offshore wintering grounds. As soon as the noise had been identified and analyzed, it was possible to screen it out with an electric filter. Then once more only the sounds of ships came through the speakers.

The great mysterious depths have withheld their secrets more stubbornly than any other part of the sea. And just because they have remained so mysterious, so eerie, so unchanging, many people have been led to suppose that some very old forms of life—some "living fossils"—may still be lurking in the deep ocean. Some such hope may have been in the minds of the *Challenger* scientists. But those hopes were not realized. The forms their nets brought up out of the deep sea were weird enough, and most of them had never before been seen by man, but they were modern types. There was nothing like the fossil trilobites or sea scorpions or great marine reptiles of past ages. All were clearly types that had developed in rather recent time.

These and other facts lead us to believe that the deep sea was not the original home of life. It has probably been inhabited for a relatively short time. While life was developing and flourishing in the surface waters, along the shores, and perhaps in the rivers and swamps, two immense regions of the earth were still too hostile for living

things. These were the continents and the deep sea. As we have seen, the immense difficulties of living on land were first overcome by colonists from the sea about 300 million years ago. The deep sea presented greater difficulties still. Its unending darkness, its crushing pressures, its glacial cold made great demands on life. Probably this region was not conquered by the higher forms until somewhat later.

Yet in recent years there have been happenings that have kept alive the hope that the deep sea may, after all, conceal strange links with the past. In December 1938, off the southeast tip of Africa, an amazing fish was caught alive in a trawl—a fish that was supposed to have been dead for at least 60 million years.

The fishermen who brought it up from a depth of only 40 fathoms realized that this five-foot, bright blue fish, with its large head and strangely shaped scales, fins, and tail, was different from anything they ever caught before. On their return to port they took it to the nearest museum, where it was christened Latimeria. It was a coelacanth, one of a very ancient group of fishes that first appeared some 300 million years ago. Fossil coelacanths had been found in rocks representing the

In the coelacanth we see a creature that has changed little in the millions of years between the age of the dinosaurs and our own time. Curiously, it survives.

next 200 million years and more of earth's history. Then the record of these fishes came to an end—apparently no more remained in the world to leave a fossil record of themselves. After 60 million years one of the group, Latimeria, appeared before the eyes of the South African fishermen! But where had these fishes been in the meantime?

The story of the coelacanths did not end in 1938. Believing there must be other such fish in the sea, a fish expert in South Africa, Professor J. L. B. Smith, began a patient search that lasted 14 years before it was successful. Then in December 1952, a second coelacanth was captured near the island of Anjouan, off the northwestern tip of Madagascar. Since then, several others have been taken.

These "living fossils" are not the only link the ocean holds with the past. Occasionally a very primitive type of shark, known from its puckered gills as a "frillshark," is taken in waters between a quarter of a mile and half a mile down. Some 50 of these sharks are preserved in the museums of Europe and America. Most were taken in Nor-

wegian and Japanese waters, but recently one was captured off Santa Barbara, California. The frillshark has many features similar to those of the ancient sharks that lived 25 to 30 million years ago. It has too many gills and too few fins on its back for a modern shark. Its teeth, also, are like those of primitive sharks. Some fish experts regard it as a relic derived from very ancient shark ancestors that have died out in the upper waters. Through this one species they are still carrying on their struggle for survival in the quiet of the deep sea.

Possibly there are other ancient creatures living out of their time down in these regions of which we know so little. But they are likely to be few and scattered. Life in the deep sea could not have stood still—it had to change and develop. For the conditions of existence in these deep waters are too unyielding to preserve life unless that life is flexible. In the great dark depths living things must mold themselves constantly to the harsh conditions. They must seize every advantage that makes survival possible in a world that is only a little less hostile than the black reaches of interplanetary space.

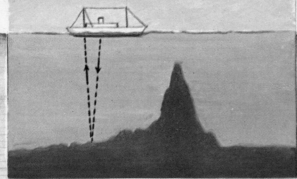

The time an echo takes to return from the bottom indicates the depth of the water. This record was taken in waters near the West Indies.

Hidden Lands

THE FIRST European ever to sail across the wide Pacific was curious about the hidden worlds beneath his ship. Between two coral islands in the Tuamotu Archipelago of the South Pacific, Magellan ordered his sounding line to be lowered. It was the line commonly used by explorers of the day, no more than 200 fathoms long. It did not touch bottom, and Magellan declared that he was over the deepest part of the ocean. Of course, he was completely mistaken. But the occasion was nonetheless historic. It was the first time in the history of the world that a navigator had attempted to sound the depths of the open ocean.

Three centuries later, in the year 1839, Sir James Clark Ross set out from England in command of two ships, the *Erebus* and the *Terror*, bound for the "utmost navigable limits of the Antarctic Ocean." As he followed his course, he tried repeatedly to get soundings, but failed for lack of a proper line. Finally he had one made on board—more than four miles long. On the third of January he obtained soundings of 2425 fathoms, showing the bottom of the ocean at that place to be, as he put it, nearly as much below the surface as Mont Blanc was above it. This was the first successful sounding of the deep sea.

But taking soundings in the deep ocean was a laborious and time-consuming task, and for a long time less was known about the hidden outlines of the ocean than about the landscape on the near side of the moon. Over the years methods improved. A strong twine was used instead of the heavy hemp line made by Ross, and later piano wire. Even with the improved gear, however, a deep-water sounding took several hours or sometimes an entire day. By 1854, when all available records were collected, there were only 180 deep soundings from the Atlantic. And by the time that modern echo sounding was developed, the total taken from all the ocean basins of the world was only about 15,000. This is roughly one sounding for every 6000 square miles!

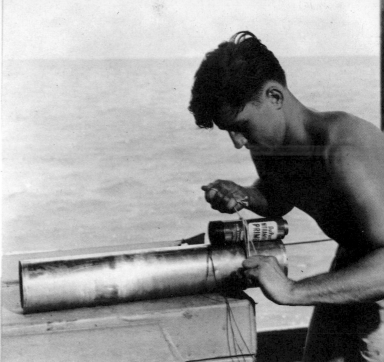

Among the most active explorers of the ocean floor are the prospectors who study sediment formations in the hope of finding deposits of oil. Here they launch a charge of explosives. A few seconds after the explosion, returning echoes will trace a profile of the sediments.

Today hundreds of vessels are equipped with instruments that trace the profile of the bottom beneath the moving ship. Soundings come in faster than they can be put on charts. Little by little, like the details of a huge map being filled in by an artist, the outlines of the ocean are emerging. But it will be years before an accurate relief map of the ocean basins can be made.

The general features of the bottom, however, are well known. Once we have passed the tide lines, there are three distinct provinces of ocean. These are the continental shelves, the continental slopes, and the floor of the deep sea. Each of these is as different from the others as a treeless plain is different from the Rocky Mountains.

The continental shelf belongs to the sea, yet of all the regions of the ocean it is most like the land.

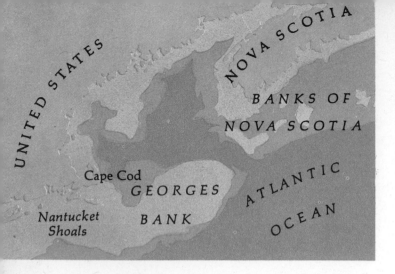

It is in the shallow waters covering the continental shelves that the great fishing grounds can be found.

Sunlight penetrates to all but its deepest parts. Plants drift in the waters above it. Seaweeds cling to its rocks and sway with the waves. Familiar fishes—unlike the weird monsters of the deep sea —move over its plains like herds of cattle. Much of its material comes from the land—for it is here on the continental shelf that the sand and the rock fragments and the rich topsoil carried by rivers are deposited. Its underwater valleys and hills, carved by glaciers, look much like the northern landscapes we know, and are strewn with rocks and gravel deposited by the moving ice sheets. Indeed, many parts of the shelf have been dry land in the past. For a slight fall of sea level has

time and again exposed it to wind and sun and rain. The Grand Banks of Newfoundland rose above the ancient seas and were drowned again. The Dogger Bank of the North Sea shelf was once a forested land inhabited by prehistoric beasts. Now its forests are seaweeds and its beasts are fishes.

Of all parts of the sea, the continental shelves are perhaps most directly important to man as a source of material things. The great fisheries of the world, with only a few exceptions, are in the waters over them. Seaweeds are gathered from their underwater plains to make scores of substances used in foods, drugs, and articles of commerce. And as the petroleum reserves of the continents are used up, geologists look more and more to the oil that may lie under these bordering lands of the sea.

The shelves begin at the tidelines and stretch seaward as gently sloping plains. No particular depth marks off the continental shelf from the continental slope—the boundary lies wherever the gentle slope changes *abruptly* to a steep one. The world over, the average depth at which this change takes place is about 72 fathoms. The greatest depth of any shelf is probably 200 to 300 fathoms, and the deepest surrounds the Antarctic continent.

Off the Pacific coast of the United States the continental shelf is nowhere more than 20 miles

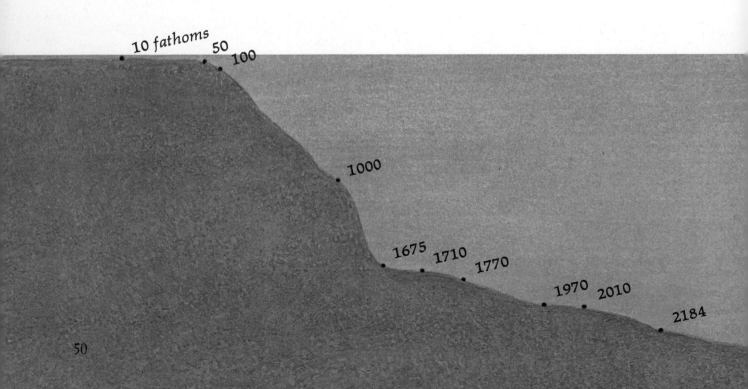

50

Generations of experience guide these fishermen to the fertile shoals of Nantucket.

wide. On the American east coast north of Cape Hatteras it is as much as 150 miles wide. But at Hatteras and off southern Florida the shelf is merely the narrowest of thresholds to the sea. This remarkable thinness may be due to the fact that the rapidly flowing Gulf Stream swings close inshore at these places and presses upon them. The shelves bordering on the Arctic are the widest in all the world—the Barents Sea shelf is 750 miles across.

The continental shelf varies greatly in width in different parts of the world. In this profile view, taken off Cape Hatteras, it is hardly more than 10 miles wide (upper left). At some point between 50 and 100 fathoms, the profile suddenly becomes steeper: this is the beginning of the continental slope. It is beyond this slope that the abyss begins.

2780   2650   2780   2800 fathoms

Millions of fishes swim among the underwater mazes of the continental shelf. These shoals are in Tuckernuck Bank, near Nantucket.

As we picture to ourselves the steeper slopes beyond the edge of the shelf, we begin to feel the mystery of the deep sea—the gathering darkness, the growing pressure, the starkness of the seascape. Here all plant life has been left behind— only a few dead husks drift down from the sunlit waters. The bottom is bare rock and clay, mud, and sand. We are in a world of animals, and the creatures, as in the deep abyss, are all flesh-eaters, preying one upon another.

These slopes are the most impressive features of all the surface of the earth. They are the walls of the deep-sea basins. They are the farthermost bounds of the continents, the true place of beginning of the sea. They are the longest and highest slopes found anywhere on earth. Their average height is 12,000 feet, but in some places they tower upward to 30,000 feet. No mountain range of the continents has so great a difference of height between its foothills and its peaks.

52

But the slopes are extraordinary for other reasons besides their steepness and height. They are the site of one of the most mysterious features of the sea—the undersea canyons. These canyons, with their steep cliffs and winding V-shaped valleys that extend a mile or more below sea level, are spectacular enough to be compared with the Grand Canyon of the Colorado. If they were not deeply hidden in the darkness of the sea they would be included in any list of the world's most exciting scenery.

The canyons have now been found in many parts of the world. Indeed, when soundings have been taken in areas now unexplored, we shall probably find that they occur throughout the world. Scientists say that some were formed quite recently, and most of them probably a million years ago, or less. But how and by what means the canyons were carved is one of the most hotly disputed problems of the ocean.

Their V-shape and the location of many of the largest ones suggests that they once had a connection with some of the great rivers of the earth today. Hudson Canyon, one of the biggest on the Atlantic coast, is separated by only a shallow sill from a long valley that wanders for more than a hundred miles across the continental shelf. If we follow the valley up (as in the illustration on the following two pages), we see that it starts at the entrance of New York Harbor and the mouth of the Hudson. Other large canyons are found off the Congo, the Indus, the Ganges, the Columbia, the São Francisco, and the Mississippi. Monterey Canyon in California, while not near a river now, is located off an old mouth of the Salinas River.

Were the undersea canyons actually cut by the rivers?

Some scientists think so. This, of course, could happen only at some time when the gorges were above the level of the ocean. But here is the difficulty. To account for the canyons by river cutting, it would be necessary to suppose that the sea level was once a mile lower than it is now. It is generally agreed that sea level was lowered at the time of the Ice Age—for then water was withdrawn from the sea and frozen in the ice sheet. Yet most scientists say that this lowered the ocean no more than a few hundred feet.

Some hold that there were heavy mud flows under the sea during the times when glaciers were advancing and the sea level was lowest. They believe this mud, stirred up by waves, poured down the continental slopes and scoured out the canyons. The canyons are young. This does seem to relate them to some happening of the Ice Age. But all the present theories leave many facts unexplained, and we have to say that we simply do not know how the canyons came into being. Their mystery remains.

So much for the slopes. Now what of the floor of the deepest region of the sea, called the abyss?

It is probably as old as the sea itself. In all the hundreds of millions of years since the abyss was formed, it has never, as far as we can learn, been drained. The abyss has always lain under the cover of miles-deep water. But this does not mean that it has not changed since the day of its creation.

Until very recent years it has been the fashion of geographers and oceanographers to speak of the floor of the deep sea as a vast and comparatively level plain. They recognized certain heights like the Atlantic Ridge. They recognized also a number of deep depressions like the Mindanao Trench of the Philippines. But they considered these as rather exceptional—as interruptions in an otherwise flat floor.

This legend of the flatness of the ocean floor was thoroughly destroyed by the Swedish Deep Sea Expedition. The expedition sailed in the summer of 1947 and spent 15 months exploring the bed of the ocean. While the *Albatross* was crossing the Atlantic towards the Panama Canal, the scientists aboard, watching the fathometer pen, were astonished at what the instruments revealed. The ocean floor was extremely rugged. Rarely were there more than a few miles of level plain together. Instead, the bottom rose and fell in curious, gigantic steps, half a mile to several miles wide. In the Pacific the profile of the bottom was so uneven that it was difficult to use many of the instruments. More than one coring tube, put down to get a sample, was left behind, probably in some deep crack in the floor of the sea.

In the Indian Ocean, however, the expedition found different conditions. Here, southeast of Ceylon, the *Albatross* ran for several hundred miles

LONG ISLAND

NEW JERSEY

Among the most dramatic features of the underwater landscape are the great canyons that cut through the continental shelf. Shown here is Hudson Canyon. Near New York Harbor (upper left) it can barely be traced as it crosses the shelf; farther out (lower right), it cuts deeply into the slope.

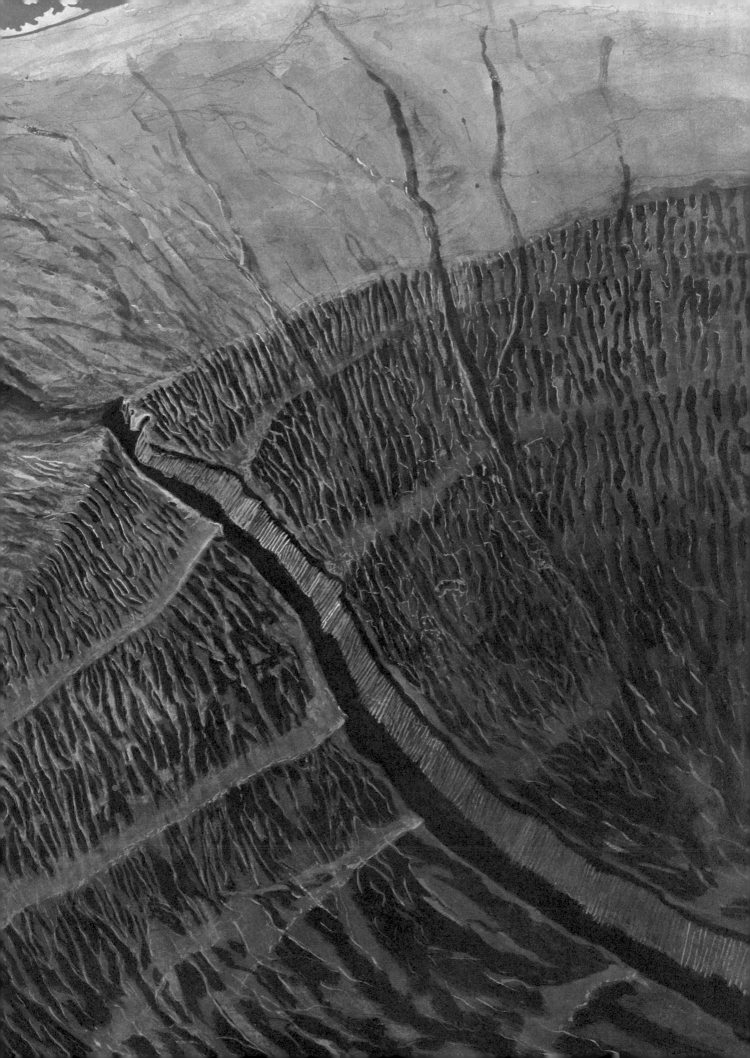

A corer being lowered into waters off California.

Where are the deepest depressions of the sea floor?

We might expect them to be in the centers of the oceanic basins. Curiously, this is not so. They are near the continents. One of the deepest trenches of all, the Mindanao, lies east of the Philippines and is an awesome pit in the sea, six and a half miles deep. The Tuscarora Trench east of Japan is nearly as deep. It is one of a series of long, narrow trenches that border the convex outer rim of a chain of islands—the Bonins, the Marianas, and the Palaus. Another group of trenches is on the seaward side of the Aleutian Islands. In the Atlantic the greatest deeps lie close to the islands of the West Indies, and also below Cape Horn, where other curving chains of islands go out like stepping stones into the Southern Ocean. And the curving island arcs of the East Indies also have their accompanying deeps.

Always these two go together—island arcs and deep trenches. And always the two occur only in areas where volcanoes are active. Rows of volcanoes line the concave side of the island arcs, while on the convex side, the ocean floor bends sharply down into deep trenches with a broad V-shape. The pattern, scientists now agree, is connected with mountain making and the sharp adjustments

across a level plain. What this bottom was made of was never learned, for the corers were broken repeatedly. But this extreme hardness suggested that the floor was composed of hardened lava rock and that the whole vast plateau might have been formed by flows from submarine volcanoes. Perhaps this lava plain is an undersea duplicate of the great basalt plateau built by lava flows in the eastern part of the State of Washington, or of the Deccan plateau of India, where the basalt lies nearly two miles thick.

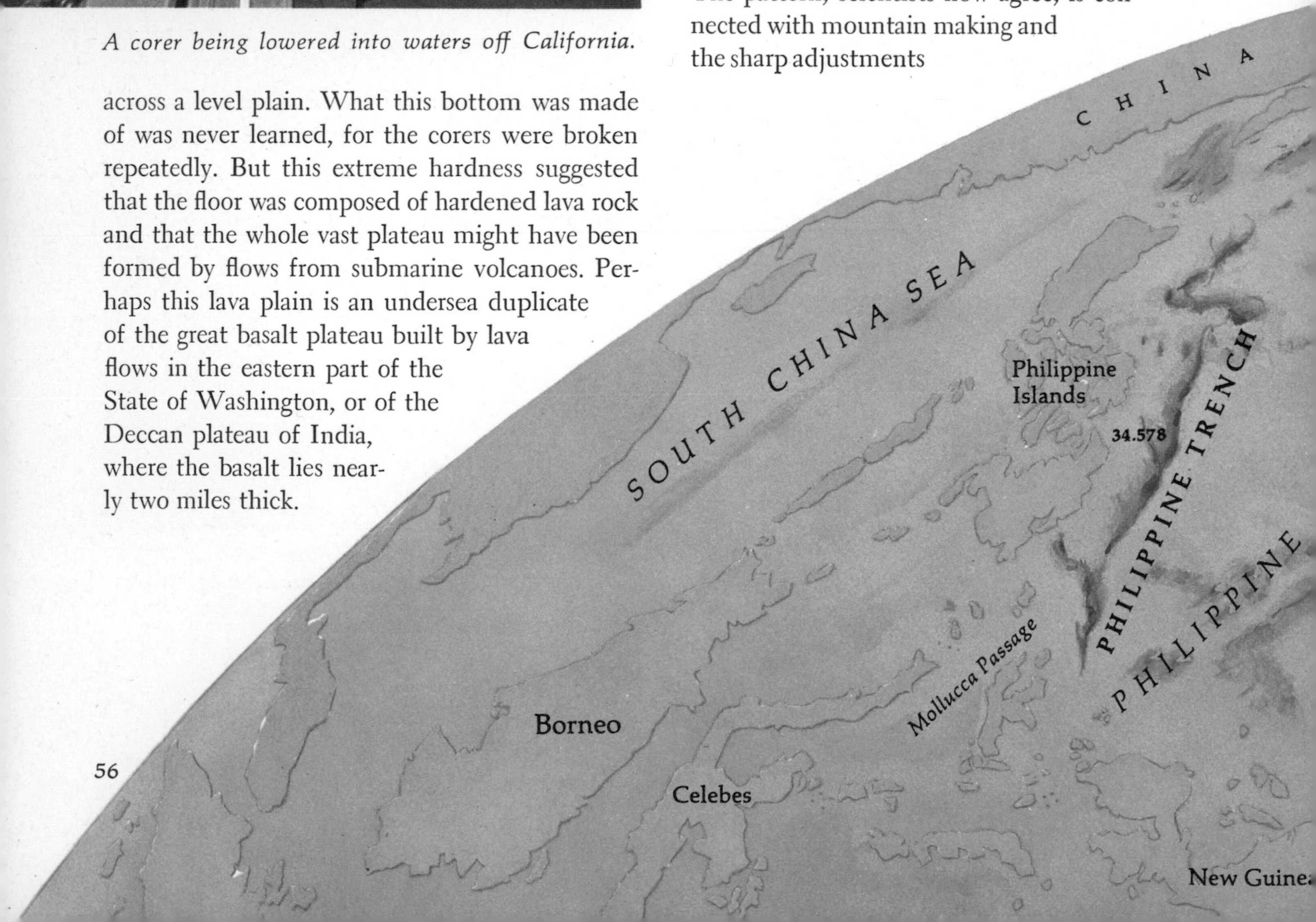

56

CHINA

SOUTH CHINA SEA

Philippine Islands

34.578

PHILIPPINE TRENCH

PHILIPPINE

Borneo

Mollucca Passage

Celebes

New Guine.

of the sea floor that go with it. The two forces seem to play against each other. The earth's crust folds upward to form mountains. It balances this by thrusting the sea floor down into the basalt underneath.

The least-known region of the ocean floor lies under the Arctic Sea. This, of course, is just what might be expected, for the difficulties of sounding here are enormous. A permanent sheet of ice, as much as fifteen feet thick, covers the whole central basin and prevents ships from coming through. Peary, in the course of his dash to the Pole by dog team in 1909, took several soundings. In 1927 Sir Hubert Wilkins, landing his plane on the ice, obtained a single echo sounding. Norwegian and Russian vessels have been deliberately frozen into the ice in order to drift with it across the basin, and such vessels have obtained most of the records for the central parts. In 1937 and 1938, daring Russian scientists landed near the Pole. Supplied

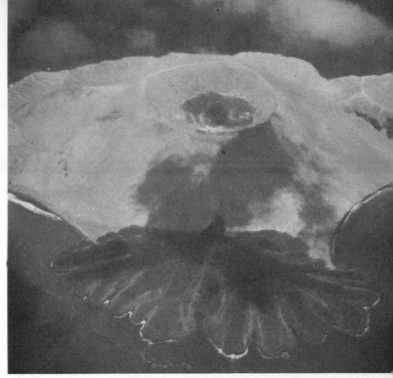

Fingers of lava stream down into the ocean from Barcena Volcano, in the Revida Gigedo islands. These islands are 400 miles west of Mexico, in the Pacific.

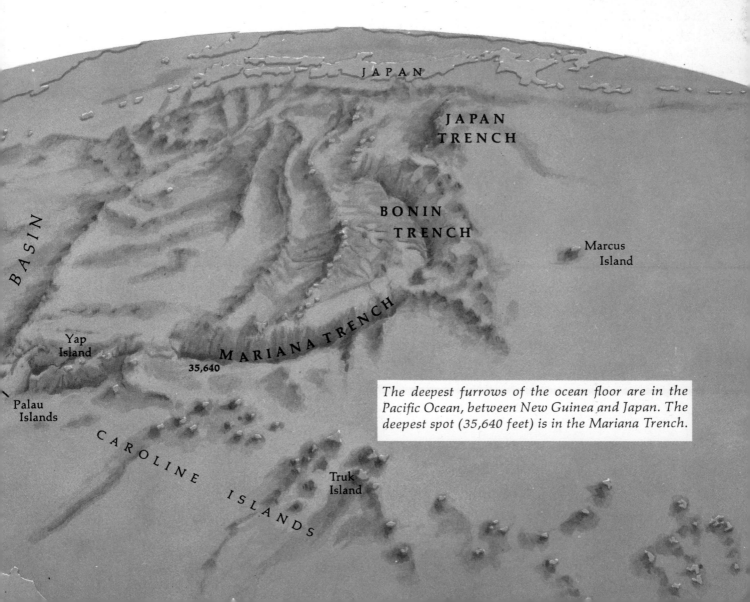

The deepest furrows of the ocean floor are in the Pacific Ocean, between New Guinea and Japan. The deepest spot (35,640 feet) is in the Mariana Trench.

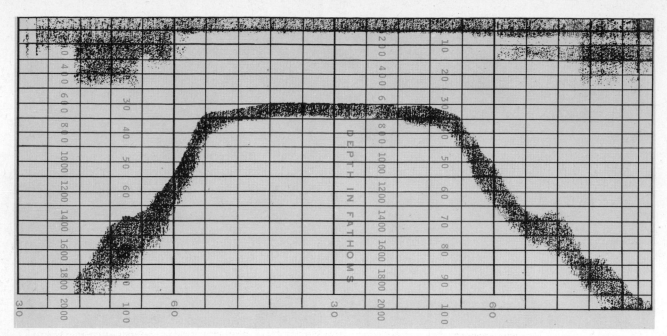

The first undersea mountain of its type ever found appears in this trace from an echo sounder. Sediments give a marked fuzziness to some parts of the outline.

by plane, they lived on the ice, drifted with it, and took nearly a score of deep soundings. But the most daring—though unsuccessful—plan for sounding the Arctic Sea was conceived by Wilkins. In 1931 he actually set out in the submarine *Nautilus* with the intention of traveling under the ice across the entire basin. Unfortunately he was prevented from carrying out the plan when something went wrong with the diving equipment.

Thus most of the top of the world is still an unsounded sea. But soon this will no longer be true. New methods of exploration, including new ways of taking soundings, are increasing our knowledge each year. For example, in 1957 a submarine of the atomic age—another *Nautilus*—spent 5½ days under the arctic ice, returning with a vast amount of information. So in time we may expect some of the most puzzling riddles of the Arctic to be solved. Among them we may get an answer to the interesting question—does the great mountain chain that divides the Atlantic end at Iceland? Or does the chain continue across the Arctic to the coast of Russia?

Since the 1940's something new has been added to maps of the sea floor. This is a group of about 160 curious flat-topped sea mounts between Hawaii and the Marianas. They were reported by H. H. Hess, a Princeton University scientist who for two years during the war happened to be in command of a United States vessel cruising in the Pacific. As Hess watched the moving pen of the fathometer, he was struck by the number of these undersea mountains. Time after time the pen would abruptly begin to rise, tracing a steep-sided mount, standing by itself. All have broad, flat tops —as though the peaks had been cut off and planed down by waves. But the tops of the sea mounts are anywhere from half a mile to a mile or more below the surface of the sea. How did they get their flat tops? Were they once above the sea? Are they "drowned islands?" It is a mystery perhaps as great as that of the submarine canyons.

Unlike the scattered sea mounts, the long ranges of undersea mountains have been marked on the charts for a good many years. The Atlantic Ridge was discovered about a century ago when surveys were first being made for the route of the transatlantic cable. Since then the Ridge has been much studied, until now we can trace the outlines of a great mountain range. The Ridge rises in mid-Atlantic near Iceland. From there it runs south midway between the continents, crosses the equa-

Almost two miles under the surface of the Atlantic Ocean lies a long chain of mountains known as the Atlantic Ridge, discovered in 1857 during the laying of a telegraph cable. The highest peaks rise from the Ridge to become islands. The only break in the Atlantic Ridge is Romanche Deep.

NORTH
AMERICA

GREENLAND

ICELAND

EUROPE

NEWFOUNDLAND

Bermudas

Cuba
Hispaniola

Nares Deep
30,246

NORTH ATLANTIC

Azores

Madeira

Canary
Islands

Cape Verde
Islands

AFRICA

St. Paul's
Rocks

Romanche Deep

Fernando
de Noronha

SOUTH

AMERICA

Brazilian

Basin

SOUTH ATLANTIC RIDGE

Angola

Basin

Rio Grande Rise

Argentine

Basin

Walvis Ridge

Falkland
Islands

South
Georgia

Tristan
da Cunha

Cape of Good Hope

Cape Horn

South Sandwich
Islands

Rising from the South Atlantic Ridge, the volcanic peak of Tristan da Cunha towers 7640 feet above the sea.

tor into the South Atlantic and goes on down to about 50° south latitude. There it turns sharply eastward under the tip of Africa and runs toward the Indian Ocean.

The Atlantic Ridge is the greatest mountain chain in the world. It is some 10,000 miles long. It is about twice as wide as the Andes and several times as wide as the Appalachians. Near the equator a deep gash cuts across it from east to west—the Romanche Trench. This is the only place at which the deep basins of the eastern and western Atlantic meet. But higher up among the peaks there are lesser mountain passes.

The greater part of the Ridge is, of course, undersea. Its central backbone rises a mile to two miles above the sea floor. Another mile of water lies above most of its summits. Yet here and there a peak thrusts itself up out of the darkness of deep water and pushes above the surface of the ocean. These are the islands of the mid-Atlantic. The highest peak of the Ridge is Pico Island of the Azores. It rises 27,000 feet from the ocean floor, the last 7000 or 8000 feet being above water. The sharpest peaks of the Ridge are the cluster of half

a dozen islets known as the Rocks of St. Paul, near the equator. The entire cluster is not more than a quarter of a mile across, and the rocky slopes of the islets drop off so steeply that only a few feet off shore the water is half a mile deep. Ascension Island is another peak of the Atlantic Ridge. Others are Tristan da Cunha, Gough, and Bouvet.

But most of the Ridge lies forever hidden from human eyes. Its shape has been made out only indirectly by the marvel of echo sounding. Bits of the Ridge have been brought up to us by corers and dredges. And some details of its landscape have been photographed with deep-sea cameras. With these aids we can picture the grandeur of the undersea mountains, their sheer cliffs and rocky terraces, their deep valleys and towering peaks.

Neither the Pacific nor the Indian Ocean has any submarine mountains that compare in length with the Atlantic Ridge. But they have smaller ranges. The Hawaiian Islands are the peaks of a mountain range that runs across the central Pacific basin for nearly 2000 miles. The Gilbert and Marshall Islands stand on the shoulders of another mountain chain of the mid-Pacific. In the eastern

60

Pacific, a broad plateau connects the coast of South America and the Tuamotu Islands. And in the Indian Ocean, a long and very broad ridge runs from India to Antarctica.

How old are the mountains of the sea? We know that on the continents mountains have been thrust up time and again only to be worn away by rain and frost and flood. What of the sea's mountains? Do they, too, begin to die as soon as they are born?

The mountains of the sea are earth's nearest approach to the "eternal hills" of which poets write. On the continents, a mountain is no sooner thrust up than all the forces of nature begin to tear it down. A mountain of the deep sea in its mature years has no such danger to face. It is beyond the reach of the ordinary forces that wear away rock. The mountain grows up on the ocean floor. It may thrust volcanic peaks above the surface of the sea. These islands are attacked by the rains, and in time the young mountain is brought down within the reach of the waves. Under the sea's attack it sinks again beneath the surface. Eventually the peak is worn down below the push and pull and drag of even the heaviest of storm waves. But here, in the calm of deep water, the mountain is secure. It will be attacked no more. Here it is likely to remain almost unchanged—perhaps as long as the earth lasts.

For this reason, the oldest oceanic mountains must be infinitely older than any ranges left on land. Professor Hess, who discovered the sea mounts, suggests that these "drowned ancient islands" may have been formed a billion years ago. If this is so, they must have reached a great age when the Appalachians were thrust up, 200 million years ago. They stood unchanged while the Appalachians were wearing down to mere wrinkles on the earth's surface. The sea mounts were old 60 million years ago when the Alps and the Himalayas, the Rockies and the Andes, rose to their majestic heights. Yet it is probable that when these, too, shall have crumbled away to dust, the sea mounts will still be standing.

As the hidden lands beneath the sea become better known, one question comes up again and again. Can the undersea mountains be linked with the fabled "lost continents"—Lemuria of the Indian Ocean, St. Brendan's Island, the lost Atlantis?

Carrying a turtle-like carapace of oxygen tanks, the television cameraman prepares for his next dive.

The legend we know best is that about Atlantis. According to the Greek philosopher Plato, Atlantis was a large island or continent beyond the Pillars of Hercules. It was said to be the home of a powerful, warlike people who raided Africa and Europe and at last made war on Athens. Then in a single day and a night Atlantis was swallowed up and disappeared beneath the sea.

Now this legend has lived on through the centuries, and as men became bold enough to sail out on the Atlantic, they speculated about where the lost continent might have been located. Various Atlantic islands have been said to be the remains of a land mass that was once far larger. The lonely, wave-washed Rocks of St. Paul, perhaps more often than any other place, have been fixed on as the remains of Atlantis. During the past century, as its great mass has become known, the Atlantic Ridge has been a lively center of speculation.

Unfortunately for these exciting theories, the Ridge can in no way be linked with Atlantis. If ever the Atlantic Ridge was exposed, it must have been a long time before there were men to people such an Atlantis. Yet, like other legends, the Atlantis story may have in it a kernel of truth. In the

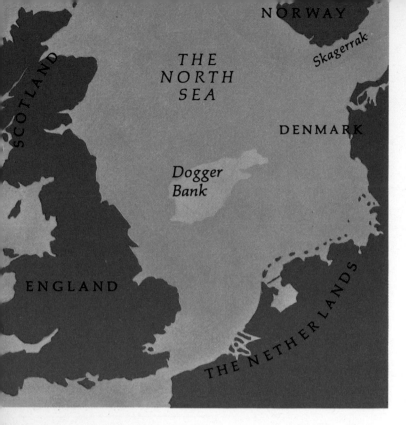

THE NORTH SEA

NORWAY

Skagerrak

DENMARK

Dogger Bank

SCOTLAND

ENGLAND

THE NETHERLANDS

For years fishermen have been trawling up strangely shaped stones from the shallow waters of the Dogger Bank. We now recognize them as the tools of Stone Age man, who lived in this area when it was dry land.

shadowy beginnings of human life on earth, primitive men here and there must have had knowledge of the sinking of an island or a peninsula. Perhaps it did not disappear so suddenly as Atlantis is supposed to have done, but it did vanish within the time one man could watch it. Those who saw such a thing happening would have described it to their neighbors and children. And so the legend of a sinking continent might have been born.

Such a lost land lies today beneath the waters of the North Sea. Only a few scores of thousands of years ago, the Dogger Bank was dry land. But now fishermen drag their nets over this famed fishing ground, catching cod and hake and flounders among its drowned tree trunks.

During the Ice Age, when immense quantities of land were locked up in the glaciers and the level of the sea went down, the floor of the North Sea for a time became land. It was low, wet land, covered with peat bogs. Then little by little the forests from the neighboring high lands must have moved in, for there were willows and birches growing among the mosses and ferns. Animals moved down from the mainland and became established on this land. There were bears and wolves and hyenas, the wild ox, the bison, the woolly rhinoceros, and the mammoth. Primitive men moved

through the forests, carrying crude stone tools and weapons. They stalked deer and other game and with their flints grubbed up the roots of the damp forest.

Then as the glaciers began to melt and floods poured into the sea, this land became an island. Probably the men escaped to the mainland before the channel had become too wide, leaving behind their lost and broken implements. But most of the animals remained till too late. Little by little their island shrank. Food became more and more scarce, but there was no escape. Finally the sea covered the island, claiming the land and all its life.

As for the men who escaped, perhaps in their primitive way they told this story to other men, who passed it down to others through the ages. At last it became fixed in the memory of the race.

None of these facts were part of recorded history until, a generation ago, European fishermen moved out into the middle of the North Sea and began to trawl on the Dogger. They soon made out the shape of an irregular plateau nearly as large as Denmark, lying about 60 feet under water, but sloping off abruptly at its edges into much deeper water. Their trawls immediately began to bring up a great many things not found on any ordinary fishing bank. There were loose masses of peat. There were many bones, and, although the fishermen could not identify them, they seemed to belong to large land mammals. Many of these objects damaged the nets and hindered fishing. So whenever possible, the fishermen dragged them off the bank and sent them tumbling into deep water. But they brought back some of the bones, some of the peat and fragments of trees, and the crude stone implements. These specimens were turned over to scientists to identify. In this strange haul of the fishing nets, the scientists recognized the animals and plants of the Ice Age and the tools and weapons of Stone Age man. Remembering how once the North Sea had been dry land, they reconstructed the story of Dogger Bank, the lost island.

The Long Snowfall

At the bottom of the world's oceans is a thick carpet of sedimentary layers that varies in composition from one place to another. In the millions of years that the sediments have been accumulating, they have left a record of the earth's history that oceanographers are now beginning to interpret.

EVERY part of earth or air or sea has a character that is its very own, a something that sets it apart from all others. When I think of the floor of the deep sea, the single overwhelming fact that grips me is the fact of the sediments that gather there. I see always the steady, ceaseless drift of materials from above, flake upon flake, layer upon layer. It has gone on for hundreds of millions of years. It will go on as long as there are seas and continents.

The sediments are the gathered flakes of the most stupendous "snowfall" the earth has ever seen. That snowfall began when the first rains fell on the barren rocks and started wearing them away. The flakes fell more heavily when living creatures developed in the surface waters and their discarded little shells of lime or silica began to drift downward to the bottom. Silently, endlessly, slowly the sediments gathered—so little in a year, or in a human lifetime, but so enormous an amount in the life of earth and sea.

In addition to the silt the rivers bring down, and the shells of tiny sea creatures, there are other things that add to the ocean's sediments. Volcanic dust, blown perhaps halfway around the earth in the upper air, comes at last to rest on the ocean and sinks. Sands are carried on offshore winds, fall to the sea, and sink. Gravel, pebbles, small boulders, and shells are dropped by icebergs and drift ice when they melt. Fragments of iron, nickel, and other materials scattered by meteorites over the sea add flakes to the great snowfall. But most widely distributed of all are the billions upon billions of tiny shells and skeletons of the smallest of all the creatures that once lived in the upper waters.

The sediments are a sort of narrative poem of land and sea. Perhaps when we are wise enough we can read it and learn the whole of earth's history. For all is written here. In the kind of materials and the manner in which they lie, layer on layer, the sediments reflect all that has happened in the

*sedimentary
layers*

bedrock

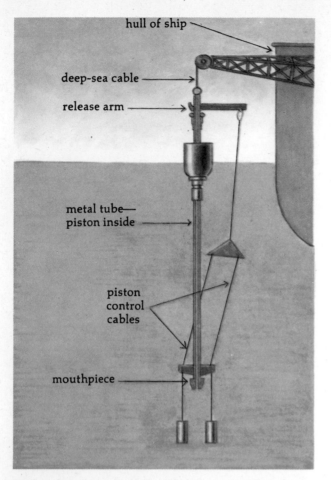

hull of ship

deep-sea cable

release arm

metal tube—
piston inside

piston
control
cables

mouthpiece

One of the corers of the Swedish Deep Sea Expedition.

waters above them and on the surrounding lands. The outpourings of volcanoes, the advance and retreat of the ice, the turning of fertile lands into deserts, the destruction of floods—all these have left their trace in the sediments.

The book of the sediments has been opened only recently, and the really exciting progress in collecting and reading samples has been made only since 1945. There was no way to get proper samples of the sediments before. We could scrape up surface layers from the sea bottom with dredges. But what was needed was an instrument like a huge apple corer, that could be driven into the bottom to remove a long sample or "core." Only in this way could the order of the layers be brought up undisturbed. Such an instrument was invented in 1935, and with the aid of this "gun" a series of cores of the deep Atlantic was obtained. These cores averaged about 10 feet long. Ten years later a much more powerful corer was developed, and now we can get cores 70 feet long. A sample as long

as that represents millions of years of history.

Another clever method for studying the sediments has been used by Professor Maurice Ewing of Columbia University and the Woods Hole Oceanographic Institution. Professor Ewing exploded depth charges and recorded their echoes. He received one echo from the top of the sediment layer. Then he received another from the bottom of the layer, or the true rock floor. That showed him how thick the layer was.

Before this method was developed, we could only guess at the total thickness of the sediments that carpet the floor of the sea. Of course, it was suspected to be vast. For thinking back through the long ages and imagining that ceaseless fall— one sand grain at a time, one fragile shell after another, here a shark's tooth, there a meteorite fragment—there was every reason to believe that the carpet must be very thick. Yet most people felt a shock of surprise and wonder when Hans Pettersson, leader of the Swedish Deep Sea Expedition, announced the *Albatross* measurements. They had been taken in the open Atlantic basin and showed the sediment layers there to be as much as 12,000 feet thick.

If more than two miles of sediments have been laid down on the floor of the Atlantic, an interesting question arises. Has the rock floor sagged under the terrific weight? Scientists hold conflicting opinions about that. But the recently discovered sea mounts perhaps offer an important piece of evidence. If the mounts are indeed "drowned ancient islands," as their discoverer believed, then they may be standing a mile or so below sea level because the ocean floor sagged.

When might this have happened? Hess—the geologist who first described the Pacific sea mounts —believed the islands had been formed long ago, before there were any coral animals in the world. For otherwise the corals would have settled on the flat, planed surface of the sea mounts and built them up as fast as their bases sank. Whether this is so or not, it is hard to see how the mounts could have been worn down so far below the waves unless the crust of the earth sagged under its load.

But to return to the sediments themselves. One thing seems probable—they have not been evenly distributed all over the ocean floor. The rains, the wearing away of the rocks, the rush of waters carrying fragments to the sea, have gone on at varying speeds in various places since the first rains fell. In the Pacific and in the Indian Ocean the Swedish scientists never found sediments thicker than 1000 feet—one twelfth as thick as in the Atlantic.

And yet we are not sure how to explain this. Perhaps the thousand feet of sediments do not represent the total thickness of the carpet. It may be that a very deep layer of lava lies under the top layer, intercepting the sound waves. It is possible that there is a second, much deeper, layer of sediments underneath the lava.

The general pattern of the sediment carpet has been known for a good many years. At the edges, around the continents, are muds that came from the land. There are muds of many colors—blue, green, red, black, and white. Farther out at sea are the oozes. They have come mainly from the sea itself—they are the remains of the trillions of tiny sea creatures.

Vast "core libraries" now exist in various parts of the world, in which hundreds of cores can be read

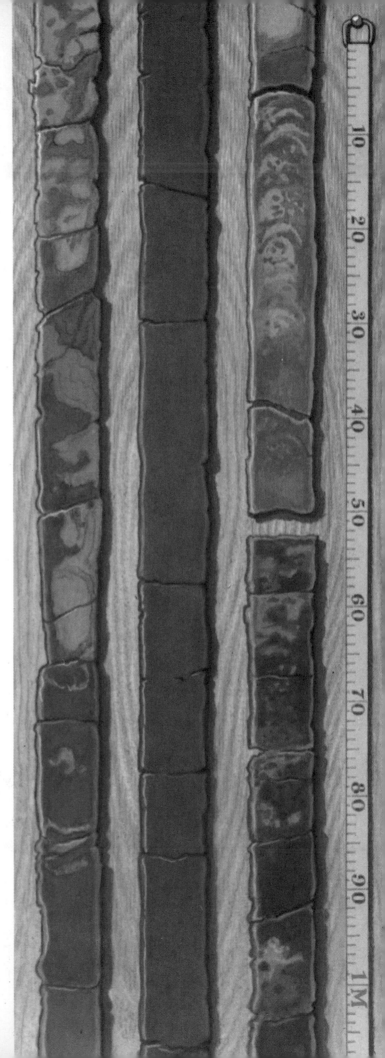

Over great areas of the temperate oceans, the sea floor is covered with the remains of one-celled creatures, of which the most abundant is called Globigerina. The shells of Globigerina are found in very ancient sediments and also in modern ones. These creatures have lived so long that over the ages the species have changed, and this makes it possible for us to date the sediments. Those with the old forms are very ancient sediments, those with the newest forms are the most recent.

Globigerina have always been very simple animals, living in a tiny shell of lime. Each shell is so small that you would need a microscope to see its details. But you must not suppose these shells to be those of animals that died. Like all one-celled animals, the individual Globigerina normally did not die, but when it reached a certain stage, it divided into two. Each time this happened, the old shell was abandoned and two new ones were formed. In warm, lime-rich seas, these tiny creatures have always multiplied at an astonishing rate. And so, although each is so tiny, their countless shells blanket millions of square miles of ocean bottom—and to a depth of thousands of feet.

The shells of Globigerina are not everywhere whole. In the greath depths of the ocean the immense pressures are too much for them. But there is another kind of shell that does reach the great depths intact. It belongs to the one-celled animals we call radiolarians. These shells look extremely delicate. They are so varied in their structure, so fragile, and so beautifully made that they remind us of snowflakes. Yet because they are made of silica, not lime, they do not break up.

There are two other sediments that are made up

of the remains of living things. One is diatom ooze. There is a broad belt of diatom ooze on the floor of the Antarctic Ocean. There is another across the North Pacific. Both are in zones where water laden with nourishment wells up from the depths. Like the radiolaria, the diatoms have coverings of silica —small, boxlike cases of varied shape and pattern.

The other ooze is found in rather shallow parts of the open Atlantic. It is made up of the remains of delicate swimming snails, called pteropods. These winged mollusks, which have transparent shells of great beauty, are here unbelievably abundant. Pteropod ooze is the usual bottom sediment in the vicinity of Bermuda, and a large patch of it occurs also in the South Atlantic.

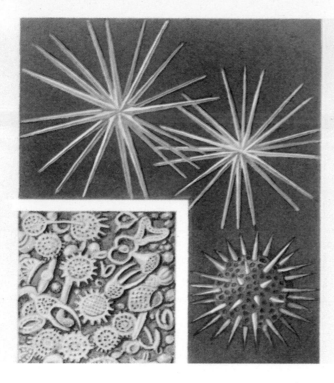

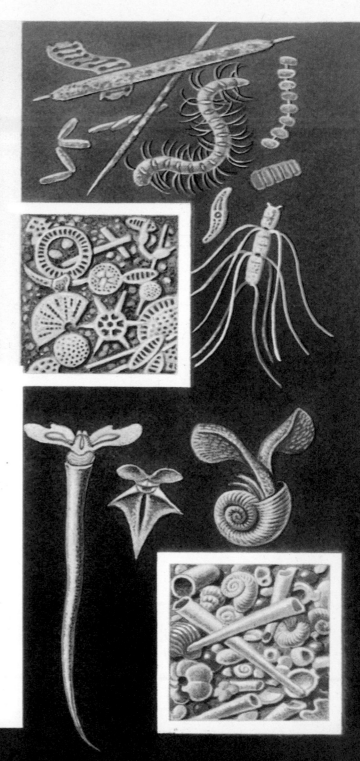

In many areas of the sea the bottom is covered with the remains of living creatures—oozes formed of minute, closely packed skeletal remains. In the square insets above are (from left to right) globigerina, radiolarian, and diatom ooze, with the corresponding live creatures beside them; to the right is pteropod ooze, next to some pteropods. Below is a landscape that might be seen at the bottom of the North Pacific, showing the hardest and most enduring remains of some larger forms of sea life—sharks' teeth and the intricate earbones of whales.

Perhaps most mysterious and eerie of all are the regions that are carpeted with red sediments in which there are no remains of life except sharks' teeth and the earbones of whales. This red clay is spread over immense areas, especially in the North

Pacific, and it occurs at great depths. This may be the reason why only the very hard sharks' teeth and whales' earbones remain whole here. It may be that all the remains that make up the other sediments are dissolved before they can reach this zone of immense pressures and glacial cold.

We have only just begun to read the book of the sediments. When more cores are collected and examined, we shall certainly puzzle out many exciting chapters. For instance, a series of cores from the Mediterranean might tell us when the Sahara Desert was formed out of the parkland that once was North Africa. Somewhere in the layers of sediment under the Mediterranean Sea there must be a layer of sand that was laid down when the hot, dry winds began to blow the surface desert sands about and carry them seaward.

The Atlantic cores that were taken within recent years have told us many interesting things. We can now look back ten thousand years or so and sense how the climate changed from age to age. For the sediment cores show us alternating layers of cold-loving and warmth-loving creatures.

From such clues we can build up a picture of the in-between periods of the Ice Age, the periods when the glaciers melted, the climate was milder, and warmth-loving creatures lived in the ocean. And we can see the periods when the sea grew chill. Then clouds gathered, snows fell, and on the North American continent the ice sheet grew. The ice mountains moved out to the coast. They reached the sea along a wide front. There the glaciers produced icebergs by the thousand. The slow-moving, majestic processions of bergs passed out to sea, and because the land was so cold, they got much farther south than any but stray bergs do today. When they finally melted, they dropped their loads of silt and sand and gravel and rock fragments that had become frozen into their under surfaces as they made their grinding way over the land. So a layer of glacial sediment came to lie over the normal Globigerina ooze. And the record of warmth and mildness was again written in the sediments.

It is exciting thus to read the story of past ages and exciting to think that just so one day the record of our own times will be read in the sediments. For the long snowfall is still in progress. Right now, in our own lifetime, the flakes of a new storm are falling, falling, one by one, out there on the ocean floor. The billions of Globigerina are drifting down, writing their record. They are testifying that this, our present world, is on the whole a world of mild and temperate climate.

Who will read their record ten thousand years from now?

Icebergs floating into temperate seas remind us of the nearness of the last Ice Age.

Bermuda, like other islands, is a mountain in the sea.

The Birth of an Island

MILLIONS of years ago, a volcano built a mountain on the floor of the Atlantic. In eruption after eruption the lava mountain grew, reaching up and up toward the surface of the sea. It came to measure a hundred miles across its base. Finally the cone of the volcano emerged as an island with an area of about 200 square miles. Thousands of years passed, and thousands of thousands. Eventually the waves of the Atlantic cut down the cone and reduced it to a shoal—all of it, that is, but a small fragment which remained above water. This fragment we know as Bermuda.

With variations, the life story of Bermuda has been repeated by almost every one of the islands that interrupt the watery expanses of the oceans far from land. For these far-off islands in the sea are fundamentally different from the continents. The continents and the ocean basins are today much as they have been throughout the greater part of time. But islands are passing things, created today, destroyed tomorrow. Nearly all have been made by volcanoes, working perhaps for millions of years to achieve their end. And it is one of the amazing things in the ways of earth and sea that a process so violent, so earthshaking, so seemingly destructive can result in an act of creation.

Islands have always fascinated people. Perhaps it is because man, who is a land animal, welcomes by instinct a bit of earth in the vast expanse of sea. Here in a great ocean basin, a thousand miles from land, with miles of water under our vessel, we come upon an island. Our imaginations can follow its slopes down through darkening waters to where

69

it rests on the sea floor. We wonder why and how it arose here in the midst of the ocean.

One thing we can be sure of—its rising was marked by a long and violent struggle. For the birth of a volcanic island is a story of ceaseless conflict between earth and sea—the forces of the earth striving to create, and all the forces of the sea opposing.

An island begins on the floor of the sea. Probably this floor is nowhere more than about fifty miles thick—a thin crust covering the bulk of the earth. In this thin covering there are deep cracks, which occurred when long ago the earth cooled and shrank unevenly. The cracks are lines of weakness in the sea floor, and the molten lava pressing upward from the earth's interior finds them the easiest places to break through. With a violent tearing of rock and a boiling of water, the lava bursts out of its underground prison.

But a submarine eruption is different from an eruption on the surface of the earth. There the lava, rocks, cinders, and gases are hurled into the

shoal, unable to emerge because it is torn down as fast as it is built up. But eventually, in new eruptions, the cone pushes up into the air. The lava hardens—and a rampart is created against the attacks of the waves.

But this does not mean that the island is permanently established. Volcanic islands often have only a short existence. Navigators' charts are marked with numbers of recently discovered submarine mountains. Many of these may be the undersea remnants of the islands of yesterday. The same charts show islands that emerged from the sea at least fifty million years ago and others that arose within our own memory. Among the undersea mountains marked on the charts may be the islands of tomorrow. At this moment they are forming, unseen, on the floor of the ocean and are growing upward toward its surface.

For the sea is by no means done with underwater eruptions. They occur fairly commonly. Sometimes the eruptions are detected only by instruments. Sometimes the most casual observer can see them. Ships in volcanic zones may suddenly find themselves in water that is violently disturbed. There are heavy discharges of steam. The sea appears to bubble or boil. Fountains spring from its surface. Floating up from the deep, hidden places where the eruption is taking place come the bodies of fishes and other deep-sea creatures, and quantities of volcanic ash and pumice.

Sometimes volcanic islands appear and disappear with amazing suddenness. Now and then there is a report of a small island where none was before. Perhaps a month, a year, five years later the island has disappeared into the sea again. About 1830 such an island suddenly appeared in the Mediterranean between Sicily and the coast of Africa. It was little more than a cinder pile, perhaps 200 feet high. Today it is a shoal, marked on the charts as Graham's Reef. Falcon Island, the top of a volcano projecting above the Pacific

air through an open crater. Here, on the bottom of the ocean, the volcano is resisted by all the weight of the ocean water above it. There is the downward pressure of perhaps two or three miles of sea water. In spite of this, the volcanic cone builds upward toward the surface. With every flow of lava it gets higher. Finally it comes within reach of the waves—but then it is attacked with even greater force. The waves violently tear at the soft ash and unhardened lava of the volcano, and for a long period the island-to-be may remain a

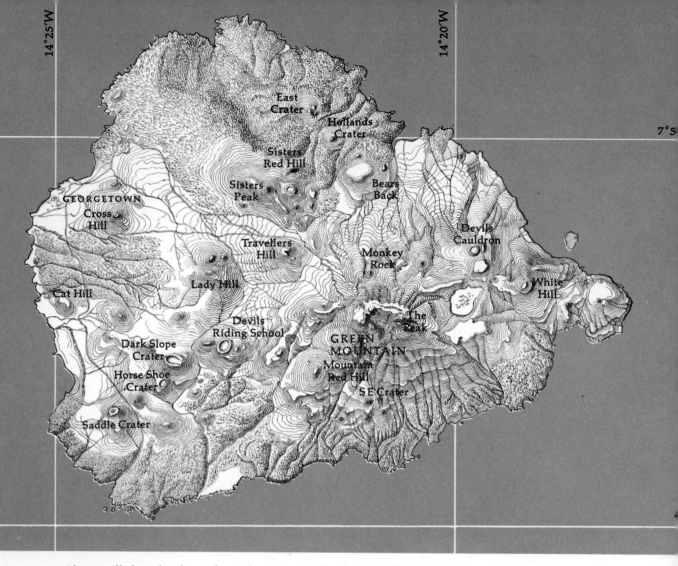

East
Crater

Hollands
Crater

Sisters
Red Hill

Bears
Back

Sisters
Peak

GEORGETOWN
Cross
Hill

Devils
Cauldron

Travellers
Hill

Monkey
Rock

White
Hill

Lady Hill

Cat Hill

The
Peak

Devils
Riding School

GREEN
MOUNTAIN

Dark Slope
Crater

Mountain
Red Hill

Horse Shoe
Crater

SE Crater

Saddle Crater

Almost all the islands of the Atlantic are volcanoes that have risen from the ocean floor.
Ascension Island, only 9 miles wide, is marked by the craters of forty extinct volcanoes.

nearly two thousand miles east of Australia, suddenly disappeared in 1913. Thirteen years later, after violent eruptions, it as suddenly rose again. In 1949 it was again reported to be missing.

The suddenness with which islands vanish points up the fact that almost from the moment it is born, a volcanic island is doomed to die. For both within and without are powerful forces of destruction. The end may be violently hastened through new explosions or landslides. Or the island may be destroyed more slowly through other forces—the rains that wear down the loftiest of land mountains, the sea, and even man himself.

Within historic times the most violent destruction of an island took place in 1883 when Krakatoa was practically torn to pieces. This was a small wooded island lying in a narrow strait between Java and Sumatra in the East Indies.

There had been an eruption on this island in 1680 and earthquakes two hundred years later. But the volcano was considered "dead." In the spring of 1883, smoke and steam began to burst from fissures in the cone. Warning rumblings and hissings came from the volcano. Then on the 27th of August, Krakatoa exploded, just as a boiler bursts when there is too much pressure of steam inside. In frightful eruptions that lasted two days, the whole northern half of the cone was carried away. The ocean rushed into the hole and added the fury of superheated steam to the boiling cauldron. When all the white-hot lava, molten rock, steam, and smoke had finally settled down, the island that once had stood 1400 feet above the sea had now become a hole a thousand feet below sea level. Only along one edge of what had been the crater did a bit of the island remain.

In its destruction, Krakatoa became known to the whole world. The noise of the explosions may have been the loudest sound ever heard on the planet. It traveled as far as the Philippine Islands and Australia. It was heard also on the Island of Madagascar, nearly 3000 miles away. A wave a hundred feet high was raised as a result of the explosions. It swept over the low-lying shores bordering the strait and carried the villages away. Tens of thousands of people were drowned. The great wave was felt on the shores of the Indian Ocean and at Cape Horn. Rounding the Cape into the Atlantic, it sped northward and continued as far as the English Channel. Clouds of volcanic dust—the pulverized rock that had been torn from the heart of Krakatoa—shot into the stratosphere. The dust was up so high that it could not at once come down. Seized by the winds that blow with more than hurricane speed at that level, the dust was carried perhaps many times around the earth. For nearly a year the sunsets all over the earth were blood-red because of that dust.

Few of the islands that disappear have a passing anywhere near so spectacular as that of Krakatoa. Some vanish without anyone's knowing for some time that they have gone. The sudden appearance of a new island may also occur without any violence and be noted merely by chance.

The Aleutians, which are the peaks of a moun-

tain chain largely built by volcanoes, are notorious for islands that come and go. It has often happened that a new island has been reported, then perhaps the following year could not be found. The small volcanic island of Bogoslof, which was first observed in 1796, has changed its shape and position several times and has even disappeared completely only to emerge again. The original island was a mass of black rock, sculptured into towerlike shapes. Explorers and seal hunters coming upon it in the fog were reminded of a castle and named it Castle Rock. Today only one or two pinnacles of the castle are left. There is a long spit of black rocks where sea lions haul out, and a cluster of higher rocks, resounding with the cries of sea birds. At least a dozen times since men have been observing this island, the parent volcano has erupted. Each time new steaming rocks have emerged from the heated waters. Some of them rose to a height of several hundred feet before they were destroyed in fresh explosions.

Nearly all the oceanic islands far from land were built by volcanoes. But the fascinating group known as the Rocks of St. Paul seems to be an exception. This group, lying in the open Atlantic between Brazil and Africa, rises as an obstruction in the midst of the racing Equatorial Current. Against these islets the seas, which have rolled a thousand miles unhindered, break in sudden vio-

A peaceful view of the island of Krakatoa, on the eve of the greatest explosion in history.

Men from the full-rigged H.M.S. Challenger *preparing to land on the bleak and barren islands of St. Paul's Rocks. Apart from the birds circling overhead, only spiders, insects, and crabs were there to greet them.*

lence. The entire cluster of rocks covers not more than a quarter of a mile, turning in a curved line like a horseshoe. The highest rock is no more than sixty feet above the sea—spray wets it to the summit. The rocks dip abruptly under water and slope steeply down into great depths. They are a puzzle. Most scientists agree that the rocks are composed of the same material as the sea floor itself. In the long distant past, we must suppose, terrific stresses in the earth's crust pushed a solid rock mass upward more than two miles!

St. Paul's Rocks are so bare and desolate that not even a lichen grows on them. And yet there are animals here—an extraordinary assortment of them. Charles Darwin saw spiders when he visited the Rocks in 1833, and forty years later the *Challenger* scientists found them still busy at their spinning. There are a few insects—some are parasites on the sea birds—and three kinds of birds that nest on the Rocks. Also there are swarms of crabs that live chiefly on flying fish which the birds bring to their young.

St. Paul's Rocks are not alone in having a peculiar set of animals—the animals and plants of all oceanic islands are amazingly different from those of the continents. Aside from animals recently introduced by man, islands far from continents are never inhabited by land mammals. There is only one exception, and that is the bat—the one mammal that has learned to fly. There are never any frogs, salamanders, or other amphibians. Of reptiles there may be a few—snakes, lizards, and turtles. But the farther the island is from a great land mass, the fewer reptiles there are, and the really isolated islands have none. There are usually a few kinds of land birds, some insects, and some spiders. The South Atlantic island Tristan da Cunha, which is as much as 1500 miles from the nearest continent, has no land animals but these: three kinds of land birds, a few insects, and several small snails.

Why is this so? Why do islands far from the principal land masses have such peculiar assortments of animals?

The reason is that they are cut off by deep water from the life of the continents. Some scientists believe that the animals came to the islands over land bridges at times when sea level was low. But this seems doubtful. For the animals that would have come over dry-shod are the very ones that are missing on oceanic islands. On the other hand, the animals and plants that we do find there are the ones that could have come by wind or water. It seems reasonable, then, to suppose that the islands were stocked by the strangest migration in the earth's history—a migration by accident, that began long before man appeared on earth and is still going on.

We can only guess how soon after an island has emerged from the sea it becomes inhabited. Certainly in its original state it is bare, harsh, and repellent. No living thing moves over the slopes of its volcanic hills. No plants cover its naked lava fields. But, little by little, living things appear. They ride in on the winds, they drift in on the currents. Rafting in on logs, floating brush, or trees, the plants and animals that are to colonize the island arrive from the distant continents.

Slightly less at the mercy of the ocean is Fernando de Noronha, on which air-borne seeds have taken hold.

The cindery slopes of Ascension scarcely seem inviting to life. But in trying to build their air-strip, American airmen found they first had to contend with the island's vast colony of nesting birds.

of the forms that inhabit oceanic islands. Spiders, which are always found on these islands, have been captured nearly three miles above the earth's surface. At such heights they might well be carried by strong winds for hundreds of miles. Seeds, too, have been collected at heights up to nearly a mile. Among those commonly taken are seeds of the so-called "thistle-down," a plant that is typical of oceanic islands.

The wide-ranging birds that visit islands of the ocean when migrating also have a good deal to do with distributing plants and perhaps even some insects and little land shells. Many plant seeds have hooks or prickles, ideal for attachment to feathers. Mud, too, clings to feathers and proves a carrier. From a ball of mud taken from a bird's plumage, Darwin raised 82 separate plants, belonging to 5 distinct species!

The Krakatoa disaster gave naturalists a perfect opportunity to observe the colonizing of an island. Most of Krakatoa had been destroyed and what remained was covered with a deep layer of lava and ash that stayed hot for weeks. This was much like a newly formed island. As soon as it was possible to visit the island, scientists searched for signs of life. Not a single plant or animal could be found. Nine months later a naturalist reported that he had discovered "one microscopic spider—only one." For a quarter of a century nothing else lived on Krakatoa except a few blades of grass. Then the colonists began to arrive—a few mammals in 1908, some birds, lizards, snakes, and various mollusks, insects, and earthworms. Ninety per cent of Krakatoa's new inhabitants, Dutch scientists found, were forms that could have arrived by air.

Man has occasionally caught glimpses of how this colonizing takes place. He has seen natural rafts of uprooted trees and matted vegetation adrift at sea more than a thousand miles from the mouths of the great rivers from which they must have come. Such rafts could easily carry an assortment of passengers. Then, too, since man has entered the upper atmosphere in his machines, he has seen how large a part the air currents must play in bringing inhabitants to the islands. Thousands of feet above the earth, the air is crowded with living creatures, drifting, flying, gliding, ballooning, or helplessly swirling along on the high winds. With special nets and traps scientists have now collected from the upper atmosphere many

76

Now, a peculiar thing has happened to the living things that in one way or another have been carried to the islands of the ocean. They have developed in a different way from the animals and plants of the continents. On the continents any species is made up of many different individuals, having many slight differences in color, shape, and habit. There is a wide choice of mates. The cross-breeding that results is a great leveler. It tends to do away with new and unusual forms and to preserve an average. On the islands it is different. Colonies are small and are cut off from the great mass of their kind. So the choice of mates is limited and a sort of inbreeding takes place. Because of this, new characteristics that develop are preserved and are passed on from one generation to the next. And an unusual form so produced on one island is not likely to arise on another. The result is that each island is the home of some species that are peculiar to it alone and are found nowhere else on earth.

It was amid the lava fields of the Galápagos Islands that young Charles Darwin got his first inkling of the great truths of the origin of species —of how, that is, the different forms of life arose. He observed the strange plants and animals and was struck by the fact that they were like, yet unlike the forms he had seen in nearby South and Central America. The giant tortoises, the black, amazing lizards that hunted their food in the surf, the birds were vaguely similar to the mainland species. Yet he was haunted by the differences. For the differences distinguished them not only from

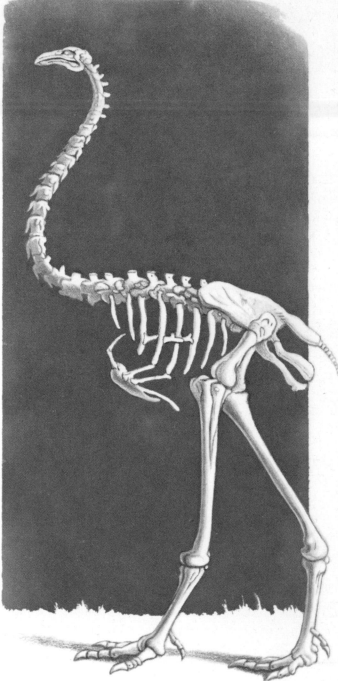

Island birds often develop in highly individual ways. Above, the skeleton of a moa, reconstructed from bones found in New Zealand; left, the dodo of the island of Mauritius, in the Indian Ocean. Though extinct for three centuries, the dodo has been seen again in recent years on a Mauritius postage stamp.

77

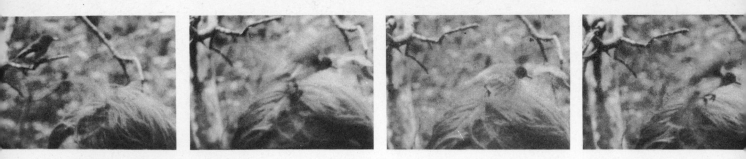

The birds of the Galápagos islands seem never to have learned to fear man.

the mainland species but also from those on other islands of the archipelago. As he viewed them, he felt himself to be on the threshold of the riddle of life. "Both in space and time," he wrote afterwards, "we seem to be brought somewhat near to that great fact—that mystery of mysteries—the first appearance of new beings on earth."

Of the "new beings" that have developed on the islands, some of the most striking have been birds. Ages before there were any human beings on earth, a small, pigeonlike bird found its way to the island of Mauritius in the Indian Ocean. There over the years this pigeon changed so that it lost the power of flight. It developed short, stout legs, and grew larger until it reached the size of a modern turkey. This was the fabulous dodo, which did not long survive the coming of man. The ostrichlike moas of New Zealand were another strange island bird—one species stood twelve feet high—and, like the dodo, the moas did not last long after the arrival of men.

One of the most interesting and delightful things that happens to island birds is that they become extraordinarily tame. When Robert Cushman Murphy visited the island of South Trinidad in the Atlantic in 1913, terns alighted on the heads of the men in the whaleboat and peered inquiringly into their faces. Albatrosses on the Hawaiian island of Laysan allowed naturalists to walk among their colonies and responded with a grave bow to similar polite greetings from the visitors. When the British bird expert David Lack visited the Galápagos Islands a century after Darwin, he found that the hawks allowed themselves to be touched. The flycatchers, yet more tame, tried to remove hair from the heads of the men for nesting material. "It is a curious pleasure," he wrote, "to have the birds of the wilderness settling upon one's shoulders, and the pleasure could be much less rare were men less destructive!"

But man, unhappily, has written one of his blackest records as a destroyer on the oceanic islands. He has seldom set foot on an island without bringing about disastrous changes. He has cut, cleared, and burned. He has brought with him the rat. And almost invariably he has turned loose upon the islands a whole Noah's Ark of goats, hogs, dogs, cats, and other destructive animals as well as plants. Upon species after species of island life, the night of extinction has fallen.

The relation of island life to its environment is in very delicate balance. When something is disturbed, the results are at once disastrous. An American specialist on birds, Ernst Mayr, tells of a steamer wrecked off Lord Howe Island east of Australia in 1918. Its rats swam ashore. In two

In the photographs on this page a Galápagos flycatcher snatches hair from a man's head for its nest.

A sailor's hat will not frighten these Galápagos hawks, who will allow themselves to be touched.

years they had so nearly exterminated the native birds that an islander wrote, "This paradise of birds has become a wilderness, and the quietness of death reigns where all was melody."

On Tristan da Cunha almost all the unusual birds that had developed there in the course of the ages were exterminated by hogs and rats. The Hawaiian Islands have become a clear example of what can happen when man upsets the balance of nature. They have lost their native plants and animals faster than almost any other area in the world.

Cattle and goats were brought to the Hawaiian Islands. They trampled and ate up the trees and other vegetation. Many of the new plants did just as much damage in their own way. A plant known as the pamakani was brought in many years ago, according to report, by a Captain Makee for his beautiful gardens on the island of Maui. The pamakani, which has light, wind-borne seeds, quickly escaped from the captain's gardens, ruined the pasture lands on Maui, and proceeded to hop from island to island. Crews of men were at one time put to work to clear it out of the Honouliuli

Galápagos birds even let one approach their young

Forest Reserve, but as fast as they destroyed it, the seeds of new plants arrived on the wind.

There was once a society in Hawaii for the special purpose of introducing exotic birds. Today when you go to the islands, you see, instead of the exquisite native birds that greeted Captain Cook, mynas from India, cardinals from the United States or Brazil, doves from Asia, weavers from Australia, skylarks from Europe, and titmice from

Japan. Most of the original bird life has been wiped out. To find any of it you would have to search hard in the farthest hills.

Most of man's tampering with nature's balance has been done thoughtlessly. But in modern times, at least, we might profit by history. About the year 1513 the Portuguese introduced goats onto the island of St. Helena, which had a magnificent forest of gumwood, ebony, and brazilwood. By 1560 or thereabouts, the goats had so multiplied that they wandered over the island by the thousand, in flocks a mile long. They trampled the young trees and ate the seedlings. By this time the colonists had begun to cut and burn the forests, so that it is hard to say whether men or goats were the more responsible for the destruction. But of the result there was no doubt. By the early 1800's the forests were gone. The once beautiful volcanic island had become a "rocky desert."

Laysan is another island that has suffered disaster because of man's tampering. It was one of the most interesting of the Pacific islands. Once it had a forest of sandalwood and fanleaf palms. There were five land birds, that existed nowhere else. One of them was the Laysan rail, a charming, gnome-like creature no more than six inches high, with wings that seemed too small, and feet that seemed too large, and a voice like distant, tinkling bells. About 1887, the captain of a visiting ship moved some of the rails to Midway, about 300 miles to the west, establishing a second colony. It seemed a fortunate move, for soon after that rabbits were introduced on Laysan. Within a quarter of a century, the rabbits had killed off the vegetation of the tiny island, reduced it to a sandy desert, and all but exterminated themselves. The destruction of the plants was, of course, fatal to the rails, and the last of them died about 1924. As for those that had been taken to Midway, their fate was no better. During the war in the Pacific, rats went ashore to island after island from ships and landing craft. They invaded Midway in 1943. The adult rails were slaughtered. The eggs were eaten and the young birds, too. The world's last Laysan rail was seen in 1944.

The oceanic islands are unique—the forms of life they have developed cannot be replaced. Men could have treated these islands as precious possessions. Instead they have wiped out in a few brief years species which it took perhaps millions of years to create. W. H. Hudson's lament for the birds of the Argentine pampas might even more truly have been spoken of the islands: "The beautiful has vanished and returns not."

A lone baby tern explores the beach that will be its home until it is ready to fly over the Pacific.

The map shows the eastern United States with labels: Lake Michigan, Lake Ontario, Lake Erie, Ohio, Appalachians, Mississippi, Alabama, Savannah, Hudson, Portland, Boston, Providence, New Haven, New York, Newark, Philadelphia, Baltimore, Washington, Richmond, Wilmington, Charleston, Savannah, Natchez, Baton Rouge, Mobile, Pensacola, New Orleans, Jacksonville, Tampa, Atlantic Ocean.

The level of the ocean has risen and fallen many times in the course of past ages. The area of the eastern part of the United States that would be flooded in a 100-foot rise in sea level today is here shaded in blue.

The Shape of Ancient Seas

WE LIVE in an age of rising seas. Along all the coasts of the United States, the gauges of the Coast and Geodetic Survey have recorded a rise in the sea level since 1930. For the thousand-mile stretch from Massachusetts to Florida and on the coast of the Gulf of Mexico the rise has amounted to about a third of a foot between 1930 and 1948. Along the Pacific shores it is slower. These records do not include the temporary changes of level caused by storms. What the records mean is .that the sea is steadily moving in on the land.

This is an exciting fact because we can seldom actually observe and measure one of the great earth rhythms within the short span of a human lifetime.

What is happening is nothing new. Over the ages the ocean waters have come in over North America many times and have again retreated into their basins. The boundary between sea and land is forever changing. The sea moves in mysterious and deliberate ways. It has its rhythms of the day, the month, and also of the ages.

Now once again the ocean is overfull. It is spilling over the rims of its basins. It fills the shallow seas that border the continents—the Barents, the Bering, and the China Seas. Here and there it has advanced into the interior and lies in such inland seas as Hudson Bay, the St. Lawrence embayment, the Baltic, and the Sunda Sea in the East Indies. On the Atlantic coast of the United States, the mouths of many rivers, like the Hudson and the Susquehanna, have been drowned by the advancing flood. Chesapeake Bay and Delaware Bay hide old, submerged river channels.

The rise so clearly noted on the tide gauges may be part of a rise that began thousands of years ago —perhaps when the glaciers of the most recent Ice Age began to melt. But it is only lately that we have had instruments to measure the advance in

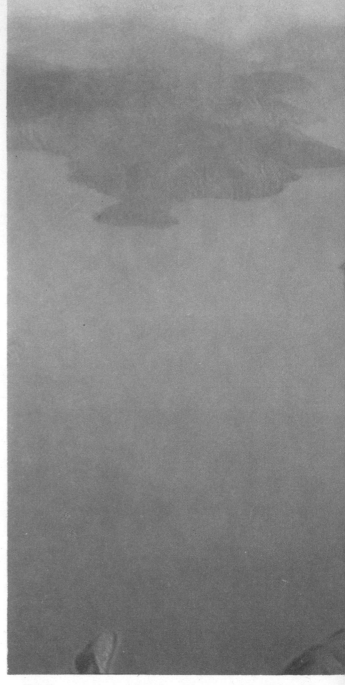

There are parts of the world where the earth, in its age, seems to have forgotten where the land ends and where the sea begins. Such a place is this area of New Zealand, in which the fiords meet the sea.

any part of the world. Even now the gauges are few and scattered, considering the world as a whole. And because world records are so few, we do not know whether the rise on our own shores is being matched on all other continents.

Where will the ocean halt? When will it begin again to retreat into its basin?

No one can say. If the rise over North America should amount to a hundred feet, most of the Atlantic seaboard, with its cities and towns, would be drowned. The surf would break against the foothills of the Appalachians. The lower part of the Mississippi Valley would be submerged.

If, however, the rise should be as much as 600 feet, large areas in the eastern half of the continent would disappear under the waters. The Appalachians would become a chain of mountainous islands. The Gulf of Mexico would creep north. In the middle of the continent it would meet the Atlantic flood that had advanced through the valley of the St. Lawrence into the Great Lakes. Much of northern Canada would be covered by water from the Arctic Ocean and Hudson Bay.

We would consider all of this extraordinary— a disaster beyond imagining. But the fact is that in the past North America and most other continents have been invaded even more widely by the sea. Probably the greatest flooding in earth's history took place about 100 million years ago. Then the ocean waters advanced upon North America from the north, south, and east. They ended by making an inland sea about 1000 miles wide. It extended from the Arctic to the Gulf of Mexico and then spread eastward to cover the coastal plain from the Gulf to New Jersey. At the height of that flood about half of North America was under water. All over the world the seas rose. They covered most of the British Isles. In southern Europe only the old, rocky highlands stood above the sea. The ocean moved into Africa. From a drowned Sweden, an inland sea flowed across Russia, covered the Caspian Sea and went on to the Himalayas. Parts of India were drowned, and of Australia, Japan, and Siberia.

With variations, this has happened again and again. Some 400 million years ago, the seas drowned more than half of North America, leaving only a few islands, large and small. Later on there were other invasions almost as great. But each time the pattern was a little different, and it is doubtful that there is any part of the continent that at some time has not lain at the bottom of one of these shallow seas.

You do not have to travel to find the sea—its traces are everywhere about. Though you may be a thousand miles inland, you can easily find reminders that will build up in your imagination the processions of its waves and the roar of its surf,

far back in time. So on a mountain top in Pennsylvania, I have sat on rocks of whitened limestone that had been made from the shells of billions of tiny sea creatures. Once they had lived and died in an arm of the ocean that overlay this place. Their limy remains had settled to the bottom. After eons of time they had been pressed into rock. Then the sea had withdrawn, and after yet more eons of time the rock had been lifted up. Now it formed the backbone of a long mountain range.

Far in the interior of the Florida Everglades I have wondered at the feeling of the sea that came to me. I wondered at it until I realized that here were the same flatness, the same immense spaces, and the same vast sky of the ocean. The masses of jagged coral rock that here and there broke the flatness reminded me that the hard rocky floor on which I stood had been only recently built by the busy architects of the coral reefs. Now the rock is thinly covered with grass and water. But everywhere is the feeling that the land has only just been won from the sea—that at any moment the sea might turn and reclaim its own.

So in all lands we may sense that once the sea was there. Marine limestone has been found even in the Himalayas, now 20,000 feet above the sea. These rocks are reminders of a warm, clear sea that once lay over southern Europe and north-

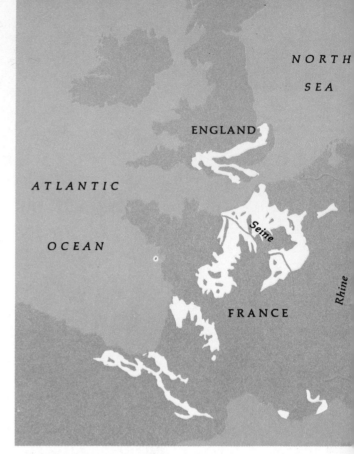

ern Africa and stretched into southwestern Asia. This was some 50 million years ago. In this sea lived immense numbers of minute creatures called nummulites. Each as it died made a contribution to the building of a thick layer of nummulitic limestone. Ages later, the ancient Egyptians quarried this rock to build their Pyramids.

The famous white cliffs of Dover are made of chalk. The chalk was laid down by the seas in that great flood of 100 million years ago. The chalk stretches from Ireland through Denmark and Germany and forms its thickest beds in south Russia.

The cliffs of Dover (top left), which on a clear day can be seen gleaming across the Strait from as far away as the French shore, are the western end of a deposit of chalk that arches over Europe to South Russia. Examined with a magnifying glass (bottom left), the chalk can be seen to be made up of millions of shells of small creatures that once lived in the sea.

It is made of shells of the tiny sea creatures called foraminifera. This chalk seems to be a shallow-water deposit. It is so pure that we must suppose the surrounding lands were low deserts. Otherwise much rock waste would have been carried seaward and would have mixed in with the chalk. At certain levels there are small, rounded lumps of flint. Stone Age men mined this flint for weapons and tools and also used it to kindle their fires.

Many of the natural wonders of the earth are due to the fact that once the sea crept over the land, laid down its deposits, and then withdrew. There is Mammoth Cave in Kentucky, for example, where one may wander through miles of underground passages and enter rooms with ceilings 250 feet overhead. Ground water, seeping down from above, was the architect that made these

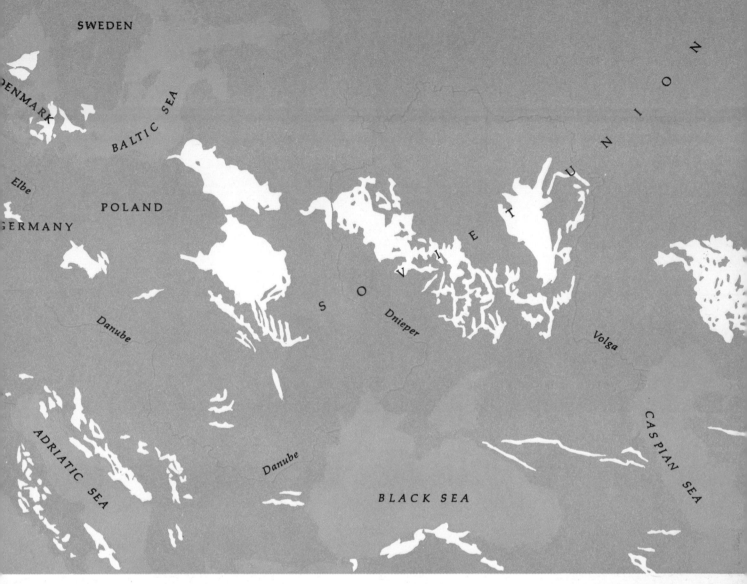

FINLAND

SWEDEN

DENMARK

BALTIC SEA

Elbe

POLAND

GERMANY

Danube

ADRIATIC SEA

Danube

SOVIET UNION

Dnieper

Volga

BLACK SEA

CASPIAN SEA

rooms and passageways. It dissolved them out of immensely thick layers of limestone laid down by an ancient sea.

In the same way the story of Niagara Falls goes far back to the time when an arm of the Arctic Sea crept southward over our continent. The sea laid down large beds of the hard rock called dolomite. In time these beds were lifted up and became a cliff. Millions of years later when glaciers melted, floods of water poured over this cliff. It was then that the Niagara River was born. It wore away the soft rocks that lay under the dolomite. The cliff was undercut. Then mass after mass of the undercut rock broke away, making the scenic gorge of the Niagara, which is still being cut today.

But what brings the ocean out of its deep basins and causes it to invade the land?

Probably there has never been any *one* cause, but a combination of causes. The warping of the crust of the earth is one. For the earth's crust is never still. With infinite slowness it moves up in one place and down in another—sometimes taking millions of years to complete the change. Each time there is a downward movement of the continental crust, the sea slowly floods the land. Each time there is an upward buckling, the water retreats.

But there are other important causes besides the warping of the crust. Every grain of sand or silt carried out and deposited at sea displaces its own volume of water. And so the sediments cause the ocean waters to rise.

"But," you might say, "the land has been wearing away ever since the first rains fell. The streams

85

have been carrying silt into the sea for hundreds of millions of years. Why hasn't the sea risen all the time?"

For several reasons. One is that as the continents are worn away, they tend to rise higher, like a ship whose cargo has been unloaded. And the ocean floor, to which the weight is transferred, sags under its load.

Then there are the undersea volcanoes that must be taken into consideration. They build up immense lava cones on the floor of the ocean. Some scientists believe these may greatly affect the changing level of the sea. For the volcanoes have great bulk. Bermuda is one of the smallest volcanic islands, but under the water it has 2500 cubic miles of rock. The Hawaiian chain stretches for nearly 2000 miles across the Pacific and contains several islands of great size. All that bulk must displace a tremendous amount of water.

The combination of causes is never the same—different ones have operated each time the sea invaded the land. In the last million years glaciers have been the chief cause. They dwarfed all others. Four times the ice caps formed and grew deep over the land, pressing southward into the valleys and over the plains. And four times the ice melted and shrank from the lands it had covered. We live now in the last stages of this fourth withdrawal. About half the ice formed in the last advance of the glaciers remains in the ice caps over Greenland and Antarctica and the scattered glaciers of certain mountains.

Now, the moisture that falls on the earth's surface as rain or snow has—directly or indirectly—all been taken from the sea. Ordinarily it is quickly returned to the sea by way of the normal runoff of rain and melting snow. But in the glacial period the summers were cool, and the snows of any win-

Kaskawulsh Glacier winds its way through the mountains of the Yukon Territory.

This entire landscape, high in the Canadian Rockies, shows the marks left by the passage of a glacier.

ter did not melt entirely but were carried over to the next winter. Then again new snows covered them. So little by little the level of the sea dropped as the glaciers robbed it of its water. And little by little the level rose when the glaciers melted.

Today, if you look in the right places, you will see evidence of some of these old high stands of the sea. On the island of Samoa in the Pacific Ocean, at the foot of a cliff wall now 15 feet above the level of the sea, you can find benches cut in the rocks by waves. You will find the same thing on other Pacific islands, and on St. Helena in the South Atlantic, and around the Cape of Good Hope. Sea caves that are now high up above the battering surf that cut them tell us clearly that once the sea was there. You will find such caves widely scattered over the world.

Of course, the marks left by the waves when the sea was at its lowest level are now deeply covered by water. They may be discovered only indirectly by sounding. But we know that during the periods when the seas sank lower and lower as the glaciers thickened, the shorelines underwent great changes. Every river felt the effect of the lowering sea. The waters speeded up and cut their channels deeper. The rivers extended their courses

87

In an era of high sea level, waves hollowed out this tunnel high on the Norwegian island of Torghatten.

over the drying sands and muds of what had only recently been the sloping sea bottom. Later, when the glaciers would melt, the streams would rush through these deep, extended channels as raging torrents. The waters would pick up great quantities of loose mud and sand and pour into the sea as a muddy flood.

The greatest advance of the glaciers in the last Ice Age took place some 200,000 years ago—well within the period when man was already on earth. Some of our Stone Age ancestors knew the rigors of life near the glaciers. To them the world was a place of storm and blizzard, with bitter winds roaring down out of the blue mountain of ice that stretched to the horizon and reached upward into gray skies. But those of our ancestors who lived half the earth away, on some sunny coast of the Indian Ocean, walked and hunted on dry land over which only recently the sea had rolled. These

men knew nothing of the distant glaciers. They did not understand that they walked and hunted where they did because quantities of ocean water were frozen as ice and snow in distant lands.

When we try to reconstruct a picture of the Ice Age, a tantalizing question arises. How low did the ocean level fall during the greatest spread of the glaciers? Did it go down 200 or 300 feet? Or did it fall ten times as much—2000 or 3000 feet?

Each of these various levels has been suggested by scientists. Perhaps it is not surprising that there should be such a wide difference of opinion. For it is only about a century since Louis Agassiz—who as a boy had lived among the mountains of Switzerland—gave the world its first understanding of the moving mountains of ice and their effect on the world. Since then, men in all parts of the earth have been patiently gathering the facts and reconstructing the Ice Age with its four advances and four retreats. And it is only the present generation of scientists that has understood that the sea level is lowered when the glaciers advance and rises when they retreat.

Most scientists think the sea level could not have sunk more than 400 feet—possibly only half as much. Of those who argue that it sank much more, most base their reasoning on the submarine canyons. The deeper gorges lie a mile or more below the present level of the sea. Around their upper parts, at least, the waters must have fallen low enough to permit the streams to cut them.

This question of how low the sea level dropped must wait until we delve further into the mysteries of the ocean. We seem to be on the verge of exciting new discoveries. Scientists of land and sea have better instruments now than ever before to probe the depths, to sample its rocks and sediments, and to read the dim pages of history they have recorded.

Meanwhile the sea ebbs and flows in these grander, more deliberate, tides whose stages must be measured not in hours but in millions of years —tides so vast that they can neither be seen nor clearly imagined by man. Perhaps we shall one day discover their final cause. We may find that it lies deep within the fiery center of the earth. Or, again, it may lie somewhere in the dark spaces of the universe.

Wind and Water

As THE waves roll in toward Lands End on the westernmost tip of England they bring with them a feeling of those distant places of the Atlantic from which they came. Moving shoreward above the steeply rising floor of the deep sea, from dark blue water into green, they roll up over the edge of the continental shelf in confused ripplings. They sweep landward over bottom that becomes ever more shallow; they break on the Seven Stones of the channel; they come in over sunken ledges and rocks that roll out glistening backs at low tide.

As they approach the rocky tip of Lands End, they pass over a strange instrument lying on the sea bottom. By their rise and fall they tell this instrument many things of the distant waters from which they have come.

If you visited this place and talked to the weather observer in charge, he could tell you the life histories of the waves that are rolling in, minute by minute, hour after hour, bringing their messages of far-off places. He could tell you where the waves were created by the action of wind on water. He could tell you the strength of the winds that produced them, how fast the storm is moving, and how soon, if at all, it will become necessary to raise storm warnings along the coast of England. Most of the waves that roll over the recorder at Lands End, he would tell you, are born in the stormy North Atlantic east of Newfoundland and

As they roll onto our shores, waves bear advance information about distant storms.

By making electrical contact at varying heights, ocean waves plot their own profile automatically.

south of Greenland. Others come from tropical storms moving through the West Indies and along the coast of Florida. A few have rolled up from the southernmost part of the world. They have taken a great-circle course all the way from Cape Horn, at the far tip of South America, a journey of 6000 miles.

Lands End is not the only place where a wave recorder is stationed. Since the end of the Second World War similar recorders have been operating on the east coast of America and on the coast of California. They are still in the experimental stage. They are not primarily intended for use on these particular coasts, for the countries bordering the North Atlantic have no need to turn to the waves for weather information—they have many weather stations placed in strategic spots. The wave recorders are being developed for use in other parts of the world, parts which have no weather information except that which the waves bring. In the southern hemisphere especially, it is expected, these recorders will be useful. For there many coasts are washed by waves that have come from lonely, unvisited parts of the ocean, parts which vessels seldom cross and which are off the normal routes of the air lines. In such remote places storms may develop unknown to anyone. They may sweep down suddenly on islands in the middle of the ocean or on exposed coasts and bring disaster. The disaster may be avoided if there is warning.

Over the millions of years, waves, running ahead of the storms, have been crying a warning. But we are only now learning to read their language. Or, at least, only now are we learning to do it scientifically. The natives of the Pacific Islands have for generations understood that a certain kind of swell signaled the approach of a typhoon. And centuries ago, when the peasants on the lonely shores of Ireland saw certain long swells, they shuddered and talked of death waves. They knew that a storm was rolling in upon their coasts.

Now our study of waves has come of age. On all sides we can find evidence that modern man is turning to the waves of the sea for practical purposes. Off the Fishing Pier at Long Branch, New

Jersey, a wave-recording instrument silently and continuously takes note of the arrival of waves from the open Atlantic. These records are carefully studied by the Beach Erosion Board of the Army Corps of Engineers, which is concerned about the rate at which the coast of New Jersey is being worn away.

Off the coast of Africa, high-flying planes recently took a series of photographs of the surf and the areas immediately offshore. From these photographs trained men determined the speed of the waves moving in toward the shore. Applying a mathematical formula, they worked out the depths off the coast—in an area where sounding in the ordinary way would have been very costly and difficult.

During the Second World War, forecasts of the state of the sea, and particularly the height of the surf, became very important when invasion was in view and men and supplies had to be transferred between boats or from boats to beaches. It was then that practical military oceanography was born. And when things didn't work out as expected, it first became frighteningly apparent how little basic information there was on the nature of the sea.

It is a confused pattern that the waves make in the open sea. There is a mixture of countless different wave trains—they intermingle, overtake, pass, or sometimes engulf one another. Each group differs from the others in where and how it was born, as well as in speed and direction. Some waves are doomed never to reach any shore, others are destined to roll across half an ocean before they dissolve in thunder on a distant beach.

Out of such seemingly hopeless confusion, the patient study of many men over many years has brought a surprising amount of order. While there is still much to be learned about waves, there is a solid basis of known facts. With these, we can put together the life history of a wave. We can predict its behavior under all the changing circumstances of its life and foretell the effect it will have on human affairs.

But what, to begin with, causes waves?

Wind is the great maker of waves. There are exceptions, such as the tidal waves sometimes produced by earthquakes under the sea. But the waves most of us know are produced by winds blowing over the sea.

Now, before constructing an imaginary life history of a typical wave, we need to know certain physical things about it. A wave has height, from trough to crest. It has length—the distance from its crest to that of the following wave. The period of the wave means the time it takes for succeeding crests to pass a fixed point. None of these things stays the same—for all depend upon the wind, upon the depth of the water, and many other matters. Furthermore, the water that makes up a wave

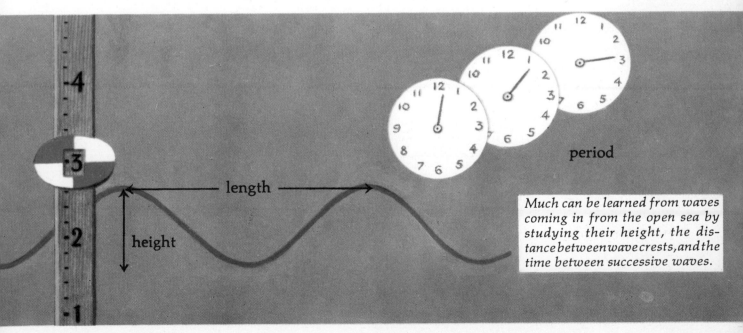

period

Much can be learned from waves coming in from the open sea by studying their height, the distance between wave crests, and the time between successive waves.

does not advance with it across the sea. Each particle of water turns around in a little circle or ellipse with the passing of the wave, but returns very nearly to its original position. And it is fortunate that this is so. For if the huge masses of water that make up a wave actually moved across the sea, navigation would be impossible.

There is another term used by those whose business it is to deal with the lore of waves—"the length of fetch." The "fetch" is the distance that the waves have run, under the drive of a wind blowing in a constant direction, without obstruction. The greater the fetch, the higher the waves. Really large waves cannot be raised in a confined space such as a bay or a small sea. Waves have to travel far to become high. It takes a fetch of perhaps 600 to 800 miles, with winds of gale velocity, to get up the largest ocean waves.

Let us see how these large waves form.

Let us suppose that, after a period of calm, a storm develops far out in the Atlantic, perhaps a thousand miles from the New Jersey coast where we are spending a summer holiday. The storm winds blow irregularly, with sudden gusts, shift-

ing direction but in general blowing shoreward. The sheet of water responds to the pressure of the winds. It is no longer a level surface. It becomes furrowed with alternating troughs and ridges. The waves move toward the coast. And the wind that created them controls their fate. As the storm continues and the waves move shoreward, their height grows under the force of the wind. They will continue to get higher and higher—but only to a point. When a wave becomes about a seventh as high from trough to crest as the distance to the next crest, it will begin to topple in foaming whitecaps. Winds of hurricane force often blow the tops off the waves by their sheer violence. In such a storm the highest waves may develop only after the wind has begun to die down.

But let us return to our typical wave, born of wind and water far out in the Atlantic. Let us assume that the wind is not so strong as to blow the top off and that the wave has merely grown to its full height. With its fellow waves it forms a confused, irregular pattern known as a "sea." Gradually as the waves pass out of the storm area, they lose height. The distance between crest and crest

This cork will remain as the waves pass by. A wave carries nothing with it, not even the water from which it fleetingly borrows its substance.

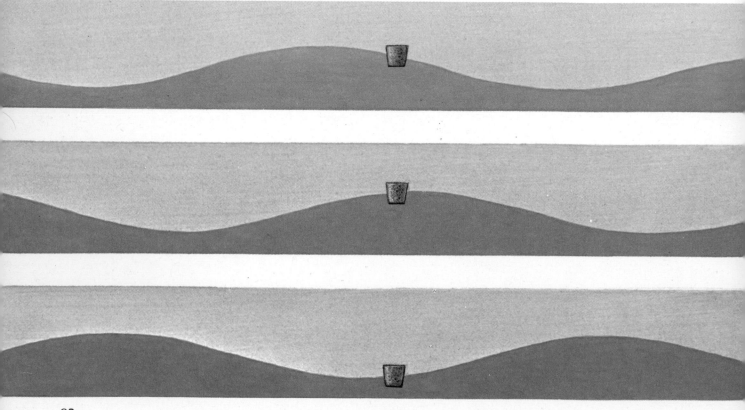

Raging winds have whipped up this heavy sea in the North Atlantic.

increases. The "sea" becomes a "swell," moving at an average speed of about 15 miles an hour. Near the coast, the pattern becomes more orderly —a series of long, evenly spaced ridges. But as the swell enters shallow water, a startling transformation takes place. For the first time in its life, the wave feels the drag of shoaling bottom. Its speed slackens. Crests of following waves crowd in toward it. Abruptly its height increases and the wave form steepens. Then with a spilling, tumbling rush of water falling down into its trough, the wave dissolves in a seething confusion of foam.

Can an observer sitting on a beach know where this surf spilling out onto the sand was born? Can he tell whether it was produced by a gale close offshore or by a distant storm?

He can at least make an intelligent guess. Young waves, only recently shaped by the wind, have a steep, peaked shape even well out at sea. From far out on the horizon you can see them forming whitecaps as they come in, bits of foam spilling down their fronts. And the final breaking of the wave is slow and deliberate. But if a wave on coming into the surf zone rears high as though gathering all its strength for the final act of its life, if the crest forms all along its advancing front and then

93

One after another, the breakers come rolling in over the even slopes of South Beach on the island of

begins to curl forward, if the whole mass of water plunges suddenly with a booming roar into its trough—then these waves are visitors from a very distant part of the ocean. They have traveled long and far before finally dissolving at your feet.

What is true of the Atlantic wave we have followed is true, in general, of wind waves the world over. They all start the same way—they respond to the force of the wind. But the incidents in the life of waves are many and their fate differs. How long a wave will live, how far it will travel, to what manner of end it will come are all determined, in large part, by the conditions it meets on its way across the sea. For the one essential quality of a wave is that it moves—anything that slows or stops its motion dooms it to break-up and death.

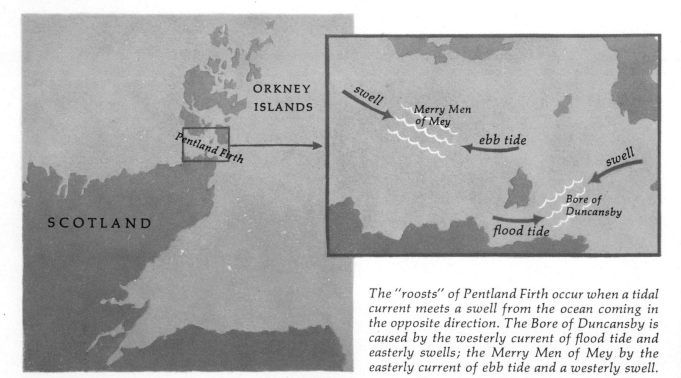

The "roosts" of Pentland Firth occur when a tidal current meets a swell from the ocean coming in the opposite direction. The Bore of Duncansby is caused by the westerly current of flood tide and easterly swells; the Merry Men of Mey by the easterly current of ebb tide and a westerly swell.

Martha's Vineyard. Here a breaker is shown in three stages of development as it plunges onto the shore.

Forces within the sea itself may affect a wave profoundly. Tidal currents may cross the path of the waves or move directly opposite to them with dire effects. Some of the most terrible furies of the ocean are unleashed this way. This is how the famous "roosts" of Scotland, like the one at the southernmost tip of the Shetland Islands, are formed. During the northeasterly winds there is no trouble. But when the wind-born waves roll in from any other quarter, they meet the tidal currents. It is like the meeting of two wild beasts. The battle of the waves and tides is fought over an area of sea that may be three miles wide when the tides are running at full strength. Vessels often become entirely unmanageable in this tumbling sea and may be tossed about for days.

In many parts of the world such dangerous waters have earned special names that have come down through the generations. The Bore of Duncansby and the Merry Men of Mey are names given to the roosts that rise at opposite ends of the Pentland Firth, to the north of Scotland, when swells from the open ocean meet tidal currents going the other way. These roosts raise a sea which, as the *British Islands Pilot* says "cannot be imagined by those who have never experienced it."

Out in the open sea, other forces may affect the waves. A train of waves may meet a hostile wind and be rapidly blown down—for the power that created a wave may also destroy it. So a fresh trade wind in the Atlantic has often flattened out the swells as they rolled down from Iceland toward Africa. Or a friendly wind, suddenly springing up to blow in the direction the waves are moving, may cause them to get higher. The waves may grow a foot or two a minute. For once a group of moving ridges has been created, the wind has only to fall into the troughs between them to push up their crests rapidly.

Rocky ledges, shoals of sand or clay or rock, and coastal islands in the mouths of bays all play their part in the fate of the waves that advance toward shore. The long swells that roll from the open ocean toward the shores of northern New England seldom reach it in full strength. They spend themselves in passing over that great undersea highland known as Georges Bank. These submarine hills and the tidal currents that swirl around and across them hinder the long ocean swells and rob them of their power. Islands scattered within a bay or about its mouth do the same. They may take so much strength from the waves that the head of the bay is free from surf. Even scattered reefs off a coast may protect it by causing the highest waves to break there, so that they never reach the shore.

Waves will be smoothed by ice crystals—here seen as they begin to form on the surface of the water.

Ice, snow, rain—all are enemies of the waves. Under proper conditions they may flatten out a sea or act as a cushion to break the force of surf on a beach. A vessel within loose pack ice may count on smooth seas although a gale is raging and surf is breaking heavily about the edges of the pack. Ice crystals forming in the sea will also smooth the waves, and snow flakes have the same effect on a smaller scale. A hailstorm will knock down a rough sea. And even a sudden downpour of rain may often turn the surface of the ocean to silky smoothness.

Oil, as every seaman knows, has a calming effect on the free waves of the open ocean. The divers of ancient times knew this and they carried oil in their mouths to release beneath the surface when rough water made their work difficult. Today instructions for using oil in emergencies are carried on most ships. But oil has little effect on surf once the waves have begun to dissolve.

In the Southern Ocean, where the waves are not destroyed by breaking on any beach, the great swells produced by the westerly winds roll around and around the world. These waves have long, unbroken crests, with great distances between

crests. We might expect to learn that the highest waves would also be found in this ocean. But this is not so. There is no evidence that the waves of the Southern Ocean surpass the giants of any other ocean. Waves higher than 25 feet from trough to crest are rare in all oceans. Storm waves may grow twice as high. And if a full gale blows long enough in one direction to have a fetch of 600 to 800 miles, the resulting waves may be even higher.

How high a storm wave can get is a much debated question. Though most textbooks say 60 feet, mariners stubbornly describe much higher waves. A French explorer reported that he encountered a wave 100 feet high off the Cape of Good Hope. Such figures are hard to believe. Yet there is one record of a giant wave which, because of the way it was measured, is regarded as reliable.

In February 1933 the U.S.S. *Ramapo*, on its way from Manila to San Diego, ran into seven days of stormy weather. The storm was part of a weather disturbance that stretched all the way

from Kamchatka to New York. It permitted the winds an unbroken fetch of thousands of miles across the Pacific. During the height of the storm the *Ramapo* kept a course running down the wind and with the sea. On the sixth of February the gale reached its height. Winds of 68 knots, or 78 miles per hour, came in gusts and squalls, and the seas reached mountainous height. While standing watch on the bridge during the early hours of that day, one of the officers of the *Ramapo* saw, in the moonlight, a great sea astern. It rose to a level above an iron strap on the crow's nest of the main-mast. The *Ramapo* was on even keel and her stern was in the trough of the sea. These circumstances made possible an exact line of sight from the bridge to the crest of the wave. Simple mathe-matical calculations based on the size of the ship gave the height of the wave. It was 112 feet.

The Ramapo, *in the early hours of February 6, 1933.*

But whatever the height of storm waves at sea, there is plenty of evidence that the leaping water from thundering breakers reaches tremendous heights. It may engulf lighthouses, shatter buildings, and hurl stones through lighthouse windows anywhere from 100 to 300 feet above the sea. Before the power of such surf, piers and breakwaters and other shore installations are fragile as toys.

Almost every coast of the world is visited now and again by violent storm surf. But there are some coasts that have never known anything else —they have never known the sea in its milder moods. "There is not in the world a coast more terrible than this!" Lord Bryce said about Tierra del Fuego on the southernmost tip of South America. There the breakers roar with a voice that, it is said, can be heard 20 miles inland on a still night. "The sight of such a coast," Darwin said of the same spot, "is enough to make a landsman dream for a week about death, peril, and shipwreck."

It seems unlikely that there exists on earth a coast where the sea waves break more wrathfully than on the Shetlands and the Orkneys. These islands lie in the path of storms that pass eastward between Iceland and the British Isles. All the feeling and the fury of such a storm are contained in the *British Islands Pilot*:

In the terrific gales which usually occur four or five times in every year all distinction between air and water is lost, the nearest objects are obscured by spray, and everything seems enveloped in a thick smoke; upon the open coast the sea rises at once, and striking upon the rocky shores rises in foam for several hundred feet and spreads over the whole country.

The sea, however, is not so heavy in the violent gales of short continuance as when an ordinary gale has been blowing for many days; the whole force of the Atlantic is then beating against the shores of the Orkneys, rocks of many tons in weight are lifted from their beds, and the roar of the surge may be heard for twenty miles; the breakers rise to the height of 60 feet . . .

That waves have the power to move rocks weigh-

ing tons need surprise no one. Experience has shown that waves can move not merely tons, but many hundreds of tons. In winter gales waves have been found with a force as great as 6000 pounds to the square foot. Perhaps it was waves of this strength that destroyed the breakwater at Wick on the coast of northern Scotland in a December storm of 1872.

The seaward end of that breakwater was a block of concrete weighing more than 800 tons. It was bound solidly with iron rods to underlying blocks of stone. During the height of this winter gale, the engineer in charge stood watching the attack of the waves from a point on the cliff above the breakwater. Before his unbelieving eyes, the block of concrete was lifted up and swept shoreward. After the storm had died down, divers investigated the wreckage. They found that not only the solid block of concrete, but the stones it was attached to had been carried away. The wave had torn loose, lifted, and moved a mass weighing not less than 1350 tons, or 2,700,000 pounds. Five years later it became clear that this feat had been a mere dress rehearsal. For the new pier, weighing about 2600 tons, was then carried away in another storm.

Keepers of lights on lonely ledges at sea, or on rocky headlands exposed to the full strength of storm surf, have recorded some of the freakish doings of the sea. A heavy ground swell was running one November day about the Bell Rock Light on the rocky coast of Scotland. There was no wind. Yet suddenly one of the swells rose above the tower, mounted to the gilded ball on top of the lantern, 117 feet above the rock, and tore away a ladder that was attached to the tower 86 feet above the water.

There have been happenings that some people regard as almost supernatural, like the one at the Eddystone Light in 1840. The entrance door of the tower had been made fast by strong bolts, as usual. During a night of heavy seas, the door was broken open *from within*, and all its iron bolts and hinges were torn loose. Engineers say that such a thing happens by sucking action. A sudden back draught was created as a heavy wave receded, and this combined with an abrupt release of pressure on the outside of the door.

On our own coasts many strange things have happened also. The 97-foot tower on Minot's

Its granite flanks towering above the raging surf Minot's Light challenges the furies of the Atlantic.

Ledge in Massachusetts is often completely covered by masses of water from breaking surf, and here a former light was swept away. Then there is the oft-told story of Trinidad Head Light on the coast of northern California. As the keeper watched a December storm from his lantern 196 feet above high water, he could see the nearby Pilot Rock engulfed again and again by waves that swept over its hundred-foot crest. Then a wave, larger than the rest, struck the cliffs at the base of the light. The wave seemed to rise in a solid wall of water to the level of the lantern and hurled spray completely over the tower. The shock of the blow stopped the turning of the light.

Not everyone can observe such dramatic happenings, but each of us on visiting the seacoast can see for himself how the waves sculpture the continent's edge. The changes brought about by the battering of the waves against the coastlines of the world are not slow like those that lead to the flooding of half a continent. The work of waves may change a coast drastically within the brief span of human life. Watching from year to year we can see the waves cut back a cliff here, there strip away tons of sand from a beach, and yet again build up a bar or a small island.

The high clay cliff of Cape Cod, rising at Eastham and running north until it is lost in the sand dunes near Peaked Hill, is wearing back about three feet a year. Already half of the ten acres which the government acquired as a site for the Highland Light has disappeared. Cape Cod is not old—it was made by the glaciers of the most recent ice age. But since the cape was made, apparently the waves have cut away a strip of land some two miles wide. At the present rate of cutting, the outer cape is doomed to disappear in another 4000 or 5000 years.

The sea's method on a rocky coast is to wear it down by grinding. The waves chisel out and wrench away fragments of rock, each of which in turn becomes a tool to wear away the lower part of the cliff. Masses of rock become undercut. Then along comes a storm and a whole huge mass falls into the sea, there to be ground in the mill of the surf and provide more weapons for the attack. On a

The waves of the Gulf of Saint Lawrence have ground out this tunnel at Rocher Percé, Quebec.

rocky shore this grinding and polishing of rocks and fragments of rocks goes on ceaselessly. It can be heard by anyone who casually strolls along the beach. For the breakers on such a coast have a different sound from those that have only sand to work with. It is a deeptoned mutter and rumble not easily forgotten.

William Henwood, who visited a British mine that extends out under the ocean, heard this surf mill from beneath the cliff and practically within the sea. At close quarters the pounding of the surf on the cliff was a terrifying sound to hear. "The heavy roll of the larger boulders, the ceaseless grinding of the pebbles, the fierce thundering of the billows, with the crackling and boiling as they rebounded, placed a tempest in its most appalling form too vividly before me ever to be forgotten," Henwood said afterwards. "More than once we retreated in affright."

The coast of Great Britain, like the coast of Cape Cod, is being attacked by "powerful marine gnawing." On the North Sea coast many British towns and villages have been lost—washed away by the sea. Old maps and records tell us where the former shorelines were. When we compare these old records with present shorelines, we are astonished by the rate at which the cliffs on many parts of the coast are being worn away—15 feet a year at one place, 19 feet at another and, at still another, up to 45 feet. No wonder one of Britain's engineers writes that "the coastline of Great Britain is not the same for two consecutive days!"

The blasting and grinding of cliffs is a very destructive process. And yet we owe some of the most beautiful and interesting shoreline scenery to it. Sea caves are almost literally blasted out of the cliffs by waves, which pour into crevices in the rocks and force them apart. Over the years the fissures widen, the rock particles are steadily removed, and a cave forms. As the water from a breaking wave is hurled upward against the roof of such a cave, it delivers blows like those from a battering ram. Eventually a hole is torn through the roof, to form a spouting horn. Or on a narrow cliff what began as a cave may be cut through from side to side so that a natural bridge is formed.

Later, after years of wearing away, the arch may fall, leaving the mass of rock to stand alone—one of the strange, chimneylike formations known as a stack.

Of all destructive waves, the ones that have fixed themselves most firmly in man's imagination are the so-called "tidal waves." People apply the term to two very different kinds of waves, neither of which has anything to do with tides. One is a seismic sea wave. The word "seismic" refers to earthquakes, and these waves are produced by undersea earthquakes. The other is an exceptionally vast wind or storm wave—an immense mass of water which is driven far above the normal high-water line by winds of hurricane force.

Most of the seismic sea waves—now called "tsunamis"—are born in the deepest trenches of

101

Wrinkled by the ripple marks of the warm currents that still flow among them, these limestone ridges off the Bahamas lie where the sea, over the years, has deposited its burden of minute skeletons and shells.

the ocean floor. Off the coasts of Japan, the Aleutian Islands, and Peru, trenches have produced waves that have claimed many lives. From ancient records to the modern newspaper, the writings of man contain frequent mention of coastal disaster caused by these great waves that rise suddenly out of the sea.

One of the earliest records is from A.D. 358. In that year a wave rose along the eastern shores of the Mediterranean, passed completely over islands and low-lying shores, left boats on the housetops of Alexandria, Egypt, and drowned thousands of people. After the Lisbon, Portugal, earthquake of 1755, the coast at Cadiz was visited by a wave said to be 50 feet higher than the highest tide. This wave came about an hour after the earthquake. In 1868, a stretch of nearly 3000 miles of the western coast of South America was shaken by earthquakes. Shortly after the most violent shocks, the sea retreated from the shore, leaving

ships that had been anchored in 40 feet of water stranded in mud. Then the water returned in a great wave, and boats were carried a quarter of a mile inland.

This withdrawing of the sea from its normal shoreline is often the first warning that a seismic wave is on the way. Thus on the first of April 1946 the voice of the breakers on the Hawaiian beaches was suddenly stilled, leaving a strange quiet. The alarmed natives could not know that this was the sea's response to an earthquake on the steep slopes of a deep trench off the island of Unimak in the Aleutian chain, more than 2000 miles away. They did not guess that in a matter of moments the water would rise rapidly, as though the tide was coming in much too fast, but without surf. The rise carried the ocean waters 25 feet or more above the normal levels of the tide.

In the open ocean the waves produced by this Aleutian quake were not outstanding, being only

102

about a foot or two high. They were enormously long, however, the distance between succeeding crests being about 90 miles. It took the waves less than 5 hours to reach the Hawaiian chain, 2300 miles away. So they must have moved at an average speed of about 470 miles per hour.

These particular seismic sea waves had one result that distinguished them from all their predecessors. After that Hawaiian disaster, people began to think that perhaps we now know enough about such waves to set up a warning system that would rob them of the terror of the unexpected. Earthquake specialists and specialists on waves and tides got together. And such a warning system has indeed been established to protect the Hawaiian Islands. A network of stations equipped with special instruments is scattered over the Pacific from Kodiak to Pago Pago and from Balboa to Palau. When an earthquake has occurred under the ocean, a warning is sent to observers at tide stations to watch their gauges for evidence that racing tsunamis are on the way. If such waves are reported to the experts at Honolulu, they can calculate when the waves will arrive at any point on the Islands. Then warnings can be issued and steps taken to evacuate beaches and waterfront areas.

The second kind of waves which people miscall "tidal waves" have a different cause. These are storm waves that sometimes rise over low-lying coast lands in hurricane zones. They belong in the class of wind waves, but unlike the waves of ordinary winds and storms, they are accompanied by a rise of the general water level, called a storm tide. The rise of water is often so sudden that it leaves no possibility of escape. Such storm waves claim about three-fourths of the lives lost by tropical hurricanes. The most notable disasters from storm waves in the United States have been those at Galveston, Texas, in 1900, on the lower Florida Keys in 1935, and on the New England coast in the hurricane of 1938. The most fearful destruction by hurricane waves anywhere on earth within historic time was in the Bay of Bengal in 1737, when 20,000 boats were destroyed and 300,000 people were drowned.

There is still another kind of great waves—usually called "rollers"—that rise now and again on certain coasts and batter them for days. These, too, are wind waves. But they are related also to change in the pressure of the air over the ocean in some area—an area that may be several thousand miles away from the beaches on which the waves will

Storm waves whipped up by a November 1945 hurricane lash the New England coast.

break. Low-pressure areas—like the one south of the Aleutians—are notorious storm breeders. The winds lash the sea into great waves. After the waves leave the storm area, they tend to become lower and longer. Then after perhaps thousands of miles of travel across the sea, they are transformed into waves known as a ground swell. These swells are so regular and so low that often they are not noticed as they pass through the short, choppy, new-formed waves of other areas. But when a swell approaches a coast and feels beneath it the gradually shoaling bottom, a change takes place. The wave begins to "peak up" into a high, steep wave. Within the surf zone the steepening becomes suddenly sharper. A crest forms, breaks, and a great mass of water plunges downward.

The west coast of Morocco, which has no protected harbor for 500 miles, has always been particularly at the mercy of swell. It has had long experience of wrecked vessels and wharves. Once the port of Casablanca was paralyzed for seven months. But in 1921 the Moroccan Protectorate established a service to predict the state of the sea, which it was possible to do because a swell travels so slowly. Now, warned that swells are approaching, ships in port get out of the surf zone and seek safety in the open sea. Modern wave-recording instruments, like those at present being tested in England and the United States, will soon provide even greater security for all such shores.

It may come as a surprise that the largest and most awe-inspiring waves of the ocean are invisible. Strangely, this is so. The greatest of all waves move on their mysterious courses far down in the hidden depths of the sea, rolling unceasingly. In the early 1900's several Scandinavian scientists called attention to these submarine waves. But another generation was to pass before science had the instruments to study them thoroughly. Now we know why it is that the vessels of Arctic expeditions often become almost trapped and can make headway only with difficulty in what is called "dead water." This "dead water" is now recognized as internal waves. Here the waves are at the boundary between a thin surface layer of fresh water and the underlying salt water.

Mystery still surrounds the great hidden waves. We do not know what causes them to rise and fall,

104

SOVIET UNION

BERING

SEA

Pribilof Islands

ALEUTIAN ISLANDS

PACIFIC

OCEAN

The area south of the Aleutians is a notorious storm breeder. Its wind-lashed waves spread to calmer regions of the Pacific, where they keep their energy but are transformed into long, low swells. On entering shallower waters off the California coast, they peak up before hurling themselves onto the land.

far below the surface. But the fact that they occur all over the ocean is well established. Down in deep water they toss submarines about, just as the surface waves set ships rolling. The internal waves seem to break against the Gulf Stream and other strong currents. Probably the invisible waves occur wherever there is a boundary between layers of different kinds of water, just as the waves we see occur at the boundary between air and sea. But the internal waves are such as have never moved on the surface of the ocean—some of them are 300 feet high!

ALASKA

CANADA

UNITED
STATES

San Francisco

There are many things we would like to learn about these great internal waves. We have only the faintest idea of their effect on fishes and other life of the deep sea. How, for instance, do the waves affect the bottom creatures of the continental slope? These creatures, it may be, are adjusted to water of a certain warmth. What happens to them when the internal waves roll in from a region of arctic cold and break against those deep, dark slopes? At present we do not know. We can only sense that in the depths of the sea are mysteries far greater than any we have solved.

Rivers in the Sea

As THE *Albatross III* groped through fog over Georges Bank all of one week in the midsummer of 1949, those of us aboard saw for ourselves the power of a great ocean current. A hundred miles of cold Atlantic water lay between us and the Gulf Stream. But the winds blew always from the south, and the warm breath of the Stream rolled over the

Bank. The combination of warm air and cold water spelled unending fog. Day after day the *Albatross* moved in a small circular room. The walls of the room were soft, gray curtains of fog, and the floor was smooth as glass. Sometimes a petrel flew across the room, entering and leaving it by passing through its walls as if by magic. Evenings the sun, before it set, was a pale silver disc hung in the ship's rigging. We could not see the Gulf Stream, but it made its great power felt,

106

and to us this was infinitely more exciting than a direct meeting with the current.

The permanent currents are one of the most majestic features of the ocean. They are controlled by vast and mysterious forces that mark out the paths to be followed by these great rivers within the sea. These forces are the spinning of the earth, the winds that deeply trouble its surface or gently caress it, and the influence of the sun and the moon.

Since the world began, the ocean currents have undoubtedly changed their courses many times. The Gulf Stream, for example, came into being only 60 million years ago. But for the brief period of man's history there has been little change. In fact, the first thing that impresses us about the currents is that they are permanent. And that they are so is not surprising, for the forces that create the currents show little inclination to change. The winds, which are the most important of these forces, blow much the same. The sun draws the earth as always and ceaselessly gives out its heat. The continents, which stand in the way of the currents and help keep them in the same place, are where they have been for millions of years.

If we could look down on the earth from another planet, we could readily see what the function of the permanent currents is. They circulate the ocean waters. The wind-driven currents at the surface of the sea are not the only ones that do this. There is also a circulation of ocean water at deeper levels, caused by the sun. For the sun heats the surface of the sea unequally—much more in the tropics than at the poles. As the water is warmed, it expands and becomes lighter, while the cold water remains dense and heavy. The heated waters of the tropics move toward the pole in the upper layers of the ocean, and polar water creeps toward the equator along the floor of the sea. But these are very slow circulating movements. They are overshadowed by the far greater sweep of the currents driven by the winds.

The winds we think of first in connection with the surface currents are the trades, the steadiest of all winds, the winds that drive the very important Equatorial Currents around the world. Under the hot sun at the equator, the air is strongly heated, becomes light, and rises. Cool air moves in from north and south of the equator to replace it—and so the trade winds are born. But the trades do not blow directly toward the equator, but diagonally from the northeast and southeast. There is an important reason for this. The spinning of the earth does a strange thing to everything that moves above its surface, whether it be a ship, a bird, a bullet, a wind, or an ocean current. Each of these tries to move directly to the place that is its target or destination. But instead it has to move in a curve, for the earth is turning all the time. When finally the moving object has got to the place it set out for, the earth has turned and carried that place away. We say that the spinning of the earth *deflects* all moving objects. In the northern hemisphere it turns them to the right. In the southern hemisphere it turns them to the left. The final result of all this on the currents is that they are slowly circulating eddies. In the northern oceans the eddies turn to the right, or clockwise. In the southern oceans they turn to the left, or counterclockwise. There are exceptions, but this is the rule.

Perhaps because the Atlantic has been crossed and recrossed by trade routes so long, its currents are known best. The Equatorial Currents were familiar to generations of seamen in the days of sail. Crossing to the Americas, they took advantage of these currents, for they run strong and their set is to westward.

There was a time, ages ago, when the North Equatorial Current went on and on to the west. It went from the Atlantic right on into the Pacific. But after the Panama ridge was formed some 60 million years ago and North and South America were joined above the sea, the Equatorial Current was shut off. It had to stay in the Atlantic. So it doubled back to the northeast and became what we call the Gulf Stream.

The Gulf Stream, too, was known to men in the days of sailing ships. As far back as the early 1500's Ponce de León chanced upon it and learned its power. Sailing south in the Gulf Stream, he found he could make no headway. Although he had a great wind, his ships "could not proceed forward but backward." A few years later, however, Spanish shipmasters learned to take advantage of the Stream. On the trip to the Americas

Labrador Current

Gulf Stream

North Equatorial Current

South Equatorial Cur

NORTH AMERICA

SOUTH AMERICA

California Current

Oyashio

North Equatorial Current

Equatorial Countercurrent

South Equatorial Current

Humboldt Current

Antarctic Current

A

East Australian Current

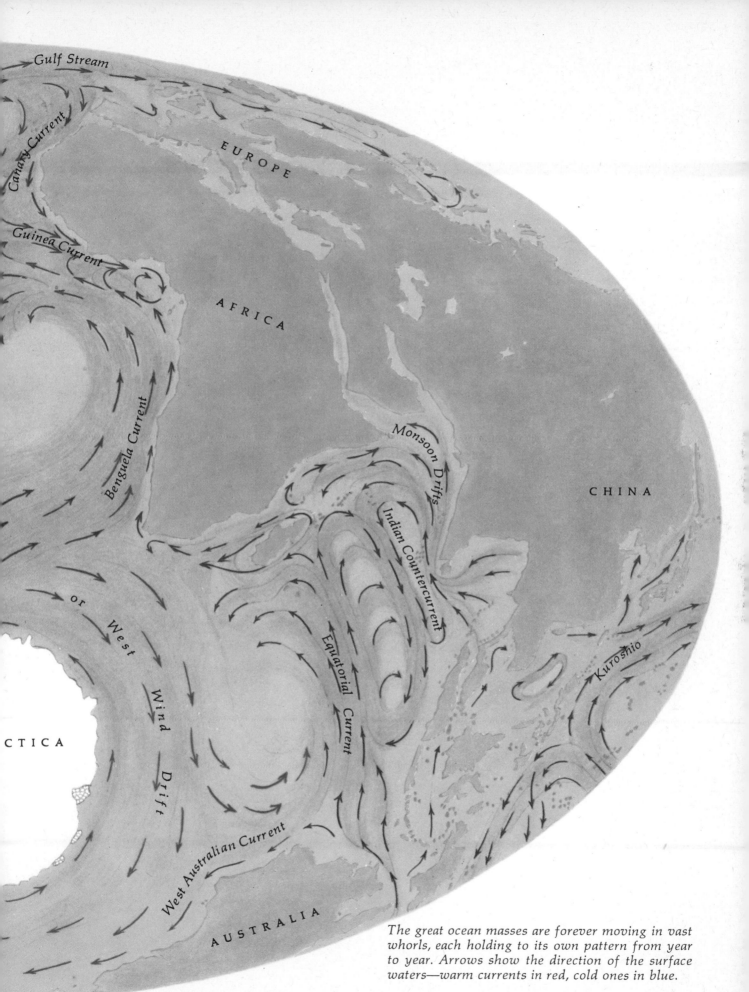

The great ocean masses are forever moving in vast whorls, each holding to its own pattern from year to year. Arrows show the direction of the surface waters—warm currents in red, cold ones in blue.

109

they would sail in the Equatorial Current, which bore them swiftly westward. Returning, they would go by way of the Gulf Stream as far as Cape Hatteras, then launch out into the open Atlantic.

American sea captains in Colonial days also became acquainted with the Gulf Stream. Yet it was not until about the year 1769 that the first chart of the current was made. It was Benjamin Franklin who asked to have it done, and the occasion of it was this:

The Board of Customs in Boston had complained about the slowness of the mail packets coming from England. It took them two weeks longer, the Board said, to make the crossing west than it did the Rhode Island merchant ships. Franklin, who was Deputy Postmaster General of the Colonies at that time, decided to find out why this was so. He went to a Nantucket sea captain, one Timothy Folger, and told him the story.

Folger thought this might well be true. He pointed out that the Rhode Island captains were well acquainted with the Gulf Stream and avoided it on the westward crossing, whereas the English captains did not.

He and other Nantucket whalers had become familiar with the Gulf Stream while pursuing whales. Whales, Folger told Franklin, kept to the sides of the current but were not met within it. So the whalers ran along the current's side. When, as often happened, they had to cross over, they sometimes met English packets in the middle of the Gulf Stream. The whalers had hailed the English captains and had tried to tell them that they were stemming a current that was against them to the value of three miles an hour and had advised them to cross it. "But they were too wise to be counselled by simple American fishermen," Folger concluded.

Franklin got Folger to mark the Gulf Stream out for him, saying it was a pity no notice had been taken of this current on the charts. He then had it engraved on an old Atlantic chart, and sent it to England. But the English captains slighted it.

It is convenient to think of the Gulf Stream as a "river" in the sea. But the great current is much grander than any river we know on the continents. Where the Gulf of Mexico narrows to form the

channel between the Florida Keys and Cuba, the Stream is as much as 95 miles wide. It is a mile deep from surface to river bed. It flows with a speed of nearly 3½ miles per hour. And it carries more water than several hundred Mississippis.

The power of the Stream is so great that even in these days of diesel engines ships show a healthy respect for it. Almost any day, if you are out in a small boat below Miami, you may see the big freighters and tankers moving south in a course that seems surprisingly close to the Keys. They are avoiding the Gulf Stream, which flows very fast here. On the land side is a wall of submerged coral reefs, to seaward is the Gulf Stream. While big boats could fight their way south against it, they would consume much time and fuel in doing

The Gulf Stream had never been mapped till Benjamin Franklin learned about it from Timothy Folger, a Nantucket sea captain. This is Franklin's chart.

110

Plate 5.

LAND

of the

ESKIMAUX'S or LABRADOR

Hudson Straits

Belle isle

NEW

GULF

of

FOUNDLAND

St. LAURENCE

St. LAURENCE

NOVA SCOTIA

C. Breton

NEW

I. St. John

Sable I.

Gᵗ   BANK

ENGLAND

of Newfoundland

NEW YORK

NEW

HAMPSHIRE

Bay of Fundy

Philadelⁱ.ᵃ

MASSACHUSETS

Cape Cod

NIA

CONNECTICUT

St. Georges Bank

NEW JERSEY

Long I.

Nantucket I

2½ Minutes

2 Minutes

LAND

Delaware

Bay

3 Minutes

Chesepeak Bay

C. Hatteras

3½ Minutes

ATLANTIC   OCEAN

Bermuda I.

A

CHART

of The

GULF STREAM

James Poupard, sculp.

The southern Atlantic coast of the United States has been shaped by the eddies set up by the Gulf Stream.

so. Therefore they choose to pick their way with care between the reefs and the Stream.

Probably the reason why the Gulf Stream flows so fast off southern Florida is that here the water is actually going downhill. This sounds strange, for we are used to thinking of the sea as being level. But this is by no means true. The winds pile up so much water in the narrow Yucatán Channel and in the Gulf of Mexico that the sea level there is higher than in the open Atlantic. At Cedar Keys, on the Gulf coast of Florida, the level of the sea is about 7½ inches higher than at St. Augustine, on the Atlantic coast.

Flowing northward, the Stream follows the sunken edge of the continent to Cape Hatteras, where it deserts the land and turns seaward. But it has left its mark behind. The four beautiful capes of the southern Atlantic coast—Canaveral, Fear, Lookout, Hatteras—have all been sculptured by powerful eddies set up by the passing of the Stream.

Beyond Hatteras, the Stream is a narrow, wandering current. Yet it is always sharply separated from the water on either side. Off the "tail" of the Grand Banks, where the Stream meets the Labra-

A blimp casts its shadow over the boundary of the warm waters (upper right) of the Gulf Stream.

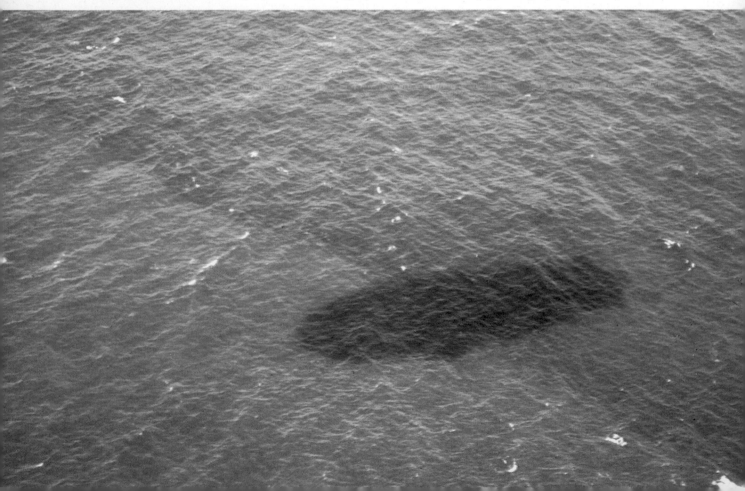

dor Current, the line is very sharply drawn. The arctic water of the Labrador Current is bottle-green, that of the Gulf Stream is indigo blue. And the difference in temperature at the boundary is startling. In winter the change is so abrupt that as a ship crosses from the Labrador Current into the Gulf Stream, her bow may be for a moment in water 20° warmer than at her stern. Naturally the air over the sea is affected by this clash of warmth with arctic cold. A thick, blanketing whiteness, one of the densest fog banks in the world, lies over the cold water of the Labrador Current.

Here, at the "tail" of the Grand Banks, where the Stream feels the rise of the ocean floor, it changes direction. It bends eastward and begins to spread out into many curving tongues. The Labrador Current itself, meantime, turns toward the mainland. The next time you wonder why the water is so cold at certain beaches of the eastern United States, remember that the water of the Labrador Current is between you and the Gulf Stream.

Passing across the Atlantic, the Stream becomes less a current than a drift of water and fans out in three main directions. Part turns southward into the Sargasso. Part courses northward into the Norwegian Sea. Part goes on eastward to warm the coast of Europe. Some of the drift passes even into the Mediterranean. From the coast of Europe it flows on, as the Canary Current, to rejoin the Equatorial Current and so closes the circuit.

In the South Atlantic, the pattern of the currents is practically the same as in those of the North, only reversed as in a mirror. The great spiral moves counterclockwise, turning to the west, south, east, north. Here the most important current is the Benguela, a river of cold water moving northward along the west coast of Africa.

In the Pacific, the North Equatorial Current is most important. It is the longest western-running current on earth—nothing blocks its way for 9000 miles from Panama to the Philippines. Meeting the barrier of the islands, most of it swings northward and becomes the warm Japan Current, Asia's Gulf Stream. The Japan Current rolls northward along the continental shelf until, like the Gulf Stream, it is driven away from the continent by a mass of icy water—the Oyashio Current.

Water from icy depths keeps the Humboldt Current cold, letting penguins live on the Galápagos Islands.

The South Pacific is so vast that we would expect it to have the most impressive of all ocean currents. But this does not seem to be true. The South Equatorial Current is so often interrupted by islands, that by the time it approaches Asia, it has lost its strength. In the South Pacific the Humboldt Current overshadows all others so far as human affairs are concerned.

This current—sometimes called the Peru—flows northward along the west coast of South America. Its water is almost as cold as the Antarctic from which it comes. But actually the chill is that of the ocean deeps. For water from the lower layers of the ocean almost constantly wells up into the current. In these cold waters, rich in minerals, there is an abundance of sea life that perhaps has no equal anywhere else in the world. Millions of Peruvian birds—principally cormorants, pelicans, and gannets—harvest this sea life. These wonderful fishermen annually consume an amount of fish that is staggering. It is equal to a fourth of the fish produced by all the United States fisheries! Man himself harvests the sea life at second hand when he gathers from the coastal cliffs and islands the bird droppings (guano), which make the most valuable fertilizer in the world.

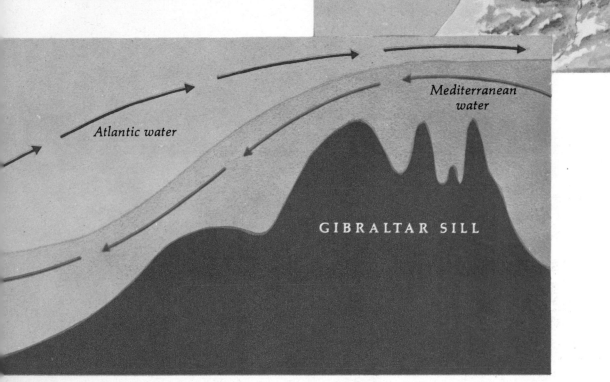

Cupped in a sheltered hollow between Africa and Europe, the waters of the Mediterranean keep their salt as their water evaporates in the sun. The heavy salt-laden waters (shown below in dark blue) pour into the Atlantic Ocean by spilling over the Gilbraltar sill, seen in profile below. As the Mediterranean water flows into the Atlantic, the lighter, less salty water of the Atlantic flows over it into the Mediterranean.

ATLANTIC

MEDITERRANEAN

Atlantic water

Mediterranean water

GIBRALTAR SILL

Leaving the coast of South America, the Humboldt Current turns westward and runs up almost to the equator. And there, about the Galápagos Islands, a strange mixture of waters occurs. The cool green of the Humboldt Current meets the blue of the equatorial waters in rips and foam lines that suggest conflicts deep in the sea. As the waters move up from below, they carry the creatures of the deeper places up to the surface, and then there takes place an amazing orgy of devouring and being devoured.

Robert Cushman Murphy, an American specialist on oceanic birds, once saw such a scene on a night when the schooner *Askoy* was off the coast of Colombia. The night had been still and dark, but the appearance of the surface made it clear

that something was going on far below the ship. All about the schooner small, steep waves leaped into being and dissolved in foaming whitecaps. Suddenly he saw a dark line, like a wall of advancing water. It seemed to be closing in on the ship. He could hear the splash and murmur of a troubled surface close by. Presently he could see a gleam of foam sprinkled with points of light on the slowly approaching swell. The dreamlike slowness of all that was going on gave him a feeling that he was not fully awake. But when the dark, white-outlined swell came close, "it proved to be nothing more than a field of dancing water, tossing its little peaks a mere foot or so into the air." Then a sharp hissing sound came out of the darkness, followed by strange sighings and puffings.

The puffers, Murphy wrote, *were blackfish, many scores, or perhaps hundreds of them, rolling and lumbering along and diving to pass beneath the* Askoy *shortly before they reached her bilge. . . . We could hear the . . . clamor of their rumblings and belchings. In the long beam of the searchlight, the hissing proved to come from the jumping of small fishes. In all directions as far as the light carried, they were shooting into the air and pouring down like hail . . .*

The surface was seething, boiling with life. . . . Larvae of clawless lobsters, tinted jellyfish, nurse chains of salps, small herringlike fishes, a silvery hatchetfish with its face bitten off, rudder fishes, hanging head downward, luminous lantern-fishes with shining light pores, red and purple swimming crabs, other creatures which we could not name at sight and much that was too small even to see distinctly . . .

A general holocaust was in progress. The little fishes were eating invertebrates or straining out the plankton; the squids were pursuing and capturing fish of various sizes; and the blackfish were no doubt enjoying the squids.

Few people see such exciting displays of upwelling. Yet these take place regularly off a number of coasts and at many places in the open ocean. Wherever upwelling occurs, it is responsible for a wealth of life, and some of the world's largest fisheries are dependent on it. The coast of Algeria is famous for its sardine fisheries. The sardines are abundant there because upward streams of deep, cold water provide the minerals to support billions upon billions of diatoms. On the west coast of the United States the catch of sardines is sometimes as much as a billion pounds in a year, making this fishery one of the largest in the world. It could not exist except for upwelling.

Water moving up from the depths is always exciting. But surface water moving down into the depths is perhaps even more dramatic—it fills us with a greater sense of awe and mystery because it cannot be seen and can only be imagined. At several known places enormous quantities of water flow downward. This downward flowing water

feeds the deep currents, of whose courses we know very little. But we do know this—they are a part of that system of balances by which the ocean pays back to one region what it borrowed from another. The North Atlantic, for example, receives quantities of water from the South Atlantic via the Equatorial Current. The return payment is made at deep levels, partly in very cold arctic water and partly in some of the saltiest, warmest water in the world—that of the Mediterranean.

So, clearly, there is no such thing as water that is wholly of the Pacific, or wholly of the Atlantic, or of the Indian or of the Antarctic Ocean. The surf that we enjoy at Virginia Beach or at Miami or at Monterey today may have lapped at the base of antarctic icebergs or sparkled in the Mediterranean sun, years ago, before it moved through dark and unseen waterways to the place we find it now. It is by the deep, hidden currents that the oceans are made one.

Driven by the wind, the sun, and the spinning of the earth, waters from distant places come to our shores.

The Moving Tides

THERE IS no drop of water in the ocean that does not respond to the mysterious forces that create the tide. No other force that affects the sea is so strong. Compared with the tide, the waves created by the winds are mere surface movements. They are felt at most no more than a hundred fathoms down. The same is true also of the planetary currents—seldom are they concerned with more than the upper several hundred fathoms.

But the tides affect the whole ocean from top to bottom. How enormous are the masses of water they move will be clear from a single example. Into one small bay on the east coast of North America —Passamaquoddy—the tidal current twice each day carries 2 billion tons of water. Into the whole Bay of Fundy it carries 100 billion tons.

What causes the tides? Why do they behave as they do?

The tides are the ocean's response to the pull of the moon and the sun. We may think of every object as exerting a pull on every other object in the universe. So in theory there is an attraction

116

Sometimes reinforcing each other's pull, sometimes counteracting it, the sun and moon together shape the earth's envelope of water.

between every drop of sea water and every star, even the one farthest away. In practice, however, the pull of the distant stars is so slight as to be lost. It is the moon and the sun that control the tides, and anyone who has lived near tidewater knows that the moon is much the more powerful. He has noticed that just as the moon rises later each day by fifty minutes on the average, than the day before, so in most places the time of high tide is later each day. And as the moon waxes and wanes, so the height of the tide varies. Twice each month, when the moon is a mere thread of silver in the sky, and again when it is full, we have the highest flood tides and the lowest ebb tides. These are called the *spring tides*, and they are highest then because at these times the sun and the moon are directly in line. They are pulling together in the same direction and bringing the water high on the beaches. Then the surf leaps upward against the sea cliffs and the boats float high beside their wharves. And twice each month, at the quarters of the moon, we have the *neap tides*. Then the sun and moon pull in different directions, at right angles to each other. At such times the difference between high and low water is less than at any other time during the month.

It is a little surprising at first that the sun, which is 27 million times as big as the moon, should have less influence over the tides than earth's small satellite. But in the laws of the universe nearness counts for more than size. The moon wields more than twice as much power over the tides as the sun.

Now this power that draws the tides lies wholly outside the earth, and so we might suppose that it acts alike all over the globe. But, curiously, it does not get the same effect everywhere. Two places just a short distance apart may have astonishing differences in tide.

When we spend a long summer holiday at the seashore, we may become aware that in our cove the tide behaves very differently from that at a friend's place twenty miles up the coast, and that it is strikingly different from what we may have known at some other spot. If we are summering at Nantucket Island, the tides will disturb our

Low tide at Cutler, Maine: the sea level drops 14 feet.

boating and swimming very little, for the range between high water and low is only about a foot or two. But if we choose to vacation near the upper part of the Bay of Fundy, we will have to adjust our water sports to a rise and fall of 40 to 50 feet. And yet both places are within the same body of water—the Gulf of Maine.

The fact is that the nature of the tide is a local matter. The moon and the sun set the water in motion, but how, and how far, and how strongly the water will rise depends on local conditions. The tide is affected by such things as the slope of the bottom, how deep the channel is, or how wide is the entrance to the bay.

The rhythms of the tide also vary. To be sure, flood tide and ebb tide everywhere follow each other just as night follows day. But there is no rule as to whether there shall be two high tides and two low each day, or only one. To those who know best the Atlantic Ocean—either its eastern or western shores—the rhythm of two high tides and two low tides seems normal. But in that great inland

117

today. They reached their greatest grandeur and power in the younger days of the earth. They will slowly grow feebler until one day there will be no tides at all.

The coming in of the tide in those far-off days when the earth was young must have been a stupendous event. For if the moon was, as we have supposed in an earlier chapter, torn from the earth, it must have remained for a time very close to its parent. During 2 billion years or more it has been pushed farther and farther away to its present position. When it was half as far away, its power over the ocean tides was not twice, but eight times as great as now. The range between high tide and low may then have been several hundred feet on certain shores. But when the earth was only a few million years old and the moon was much nearer still, the sweep of the tides must have been beyond imagining. Twice each day, the fury of the incoming waters would drown the margins of the continents. The waves would batter the crests of high cliffs and sweep inland to wear away the continents.

Such tides alone must have been enough to prevent any living thing from getting a foothold on the land. And had not conditions changed, it is reasonable to suppose that life would have developed no further than the fishes. But over the millions of years the moon has moved away. It has been driven off by the very tides it creates.

For the drag of the waters over the bed of the ocean, and over the shallow edges of the continents, and over the inland seas, acts like a brake. It slows down the earth in its turning. And as the earth slows down, the spinning of the moon speeds up and it is also carried farther away. In those early days we have spoken of, it took the earth perhaps only about 4 hours to turn on its axis—that is, a day was only 4 hours long. Since then, the spinning of the globe, as everyone knows, has been so greatly slowed that it takes the earth about 24 hours to make a complete rotation. This slowing down will go on, the mathematicians tell us, until the day is about 50 times as long as now—when there will be 1200 hours in a day. As the moon moves away,

sea, the Gulf of Mexico, there is a different rhythm —around most of its borders there is but one rise and one fall. This "diurnal" rhythm is found in scattered places about the earth—at St. Michael, Alaska, for instance. But by far the greater part of the world's coasts, including most of the Pacific basin, has a mixture of the two types of tides. There are two high and two low tides in a day, but either the two highs or the two lows are very unequal.

The tides have not always been as they are

In the farthest inland corner of the Bay of Saint Malo, between Brittany and Normandy, stands the fortified rock of Mont Saint Michel, surmounted by its ancient abbey. Here we see it standing alone amid the sands at low tide.

The tide of the bay has now crept up, covering the mudflats and the sands. Only the mile-long causeway now links the island with the mainland of France. The tidal range here is among the greatest in the world, often reaching 40 feet.

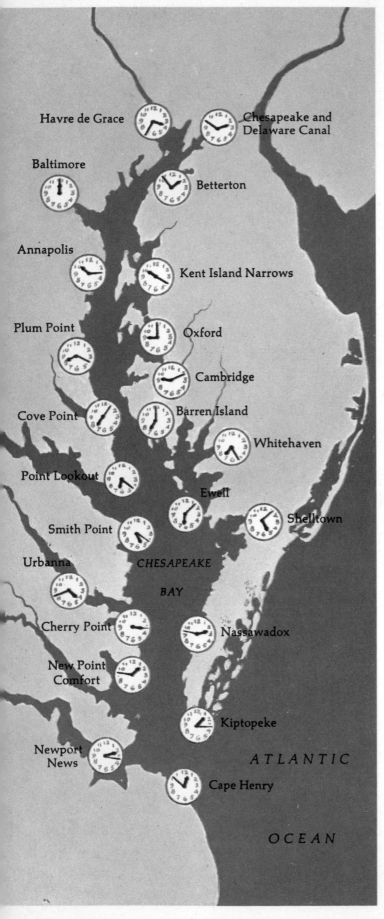

Havre de Grace

Chesapeake and
Delaware Canal

Baltimore

Betterton

Annapolis

Kent Island Narrows

Plum Point

Oxford

Cambridge

Cove Point

Barren Island

Whitehaven

Point Lookout

Ewell

Smith Point

Shelltown

Urbanna

CHESAPEAKE

BAY

Cherry Point

Nassawadox

New Point
Comfort

Kiptopeke

Newport
News

ATLANTIC

Cape Henry

OCEAN

The water level of Chesapeake Bay rises and falls twice daily with the tides. But high tide occurs more than twelve hours earlier at the entrance of the bay than it does at Betterton at the far northern end.

it will have less power over the tides, and they will grow weaker. Also, as the moon moves away, it will take it longer to get around the earth. When finally it takes the earth as long to make a complete turn on its axis as it takes the moon to get around it—that is, when the day and the month are equal—then the moon will lose its power over the tides and there will be no more of them. So the mathematicians have worked it out.

All this, of course, will require a vast amount of time, and before it comes to pass, it is quite probable that the human race will have vanished from the earth. Yet the brake which the tides are putting on the earth is slowing it down fast enough to be measured. Our ordinary clocks, geared to the earth's rotation, cannot, of course, show the lengthening day. But the new atomic clocks now in the making will show actual time and will differ from other clocks. Our day is believed to be now several seconds longer than it was in the days when the ancient Egyptians built their Pyramids. The atomic clocks will show such tiny changes in earthly time.

As we have said, the tides have become tamer. We now measure their range in tens instead of hundreds of feet. Nevertheless, mariners are greatly concerned with the stages of the tide, the direction of the tidal currents, and also with the violent indirect effects of the tides.

Nothing the human mind has invented can tame a tide rip or control the rhythm of ebb and flow. The most modern instruments cannot carry a vessel over a shoal until the tide has brought enough water over it. Even the *Queen Mary* waits for slack water to come to her pier in New York—otherwise the set of the tidal current might swing her against the pier with enough force to crush it. In some of the ports on the Bay of Fundy the tides entirely control loading and unloading of cargoes. For on account of the great range of tide, vessels can come to the docks during only a few hours on each tide. And they must leave very promptly, too, or they will be stranded in mud at low water.

In narrow passages, tidal currents often move with such violence that they are a menace to navigation. Certain of these passages are among the most dangerous waterways in the world. When entering Bering Sea through the Straits, vessels are sometimes thrown against the rocks by the force of the tide. Through Akun Strait, the flood pours like a mountain torrent, causing high seas to sweep the decks. There a 15-foot wave of a tide rip may suddenly rise and sweep across a vessel—and more than one man has been carried off to his death in this way.

On the opposite side of the world, the tide from the open Atlantic presses eastward between the islands of the Shetlands and Orkneys into the North Sea. On the ebb it returns through the same narrow passages. At certain stages of the tide the waters dome up in some places, in others they form pits, while dangerous eddies dot the passages. Even in calm weather boats are warned to avoid the eddies of Pentland Firth, which are known as the Swilkie. With an ebb tide and a northwest wind, the heavy, breaking seas of the Swilkie are such a threat to the vessels that few sailors, having once met them, would be rash enough to meet again.

Edgar Allan Poe built a weird and wonderful tale out of one of the grim terrors of the tide.

Few who have read *Descent into the Maelstrom* will forget the story. He tells how an old man led his companion to a mountain cliff high above the sea and let him watch the water far below in the narrow passageway between the islands. The water foamed and bubbled and boiled until suddenly a whirlpool was formed before their eyes and rushed with an appalling sound through the narrow waterway. Then the old man related how he had once gone down into the whirlpool and miraculously escaped from it.

Most of us have wondered how much of the story was fact and how much came from Poe's imagination. But there actually is a Maelstrom. And it is just where Poe placed it—between two of the islands of the Lofoten group, off the west coast of Norway. It is, as he described it, a gigantic whirlpool or series of whirlpools, and men with their boats have actually been drawn down into these spinning funnels of water. Poe exaggerates certain details. But the essential facts are true.

The whirlpools, or Malström, are cavities in the form of an inverted bell, wide and rounded at the mouth and narrowed toward the bottom. They are largest when first formed and are carried along with the current. Gradually they get smaller until they disappear. But before one does disappear, as

Rushing tidal waters can form dangerous eddies, such as the Maelstrom off the Norwegian coast.

121

of the flood tide enters the river as a single wave with a steep and high front. Sometimes two or three waves follow each other. These bores form only where there is a wide range between high and low tide and where sand bars or islands in the mouth of the river get in the way of the incoming waters. They hold back the tide until it finally gathers itself together and rushes through up the river.

The Amazon has a bore that is remarkable for the distance it travels upstream. It goes up some 200 miles. On the Tsientang River, which empties into the China Sea just south of Shanghai, the bore controls all shipping. This is the largest, most dangerous, and best known bore in the world, and, it is said, the ancient Chinese used to throw offerings into the river to appease its angry spirit. During most of the month the bore comes up the river in a wave 8 to 11 feet high, moving in at a speed of 12 or 13 knots. Its front is a sloping cascade of bubbling foam that falls forward and pounds on itself and on the river. At the spring tides of the full moon and the new moon it is fiercest, and then the advancing wave is said to rise 25 feet above the surface of the river.

Not only man is affected by the tides. Their in-

many as three more are born, following each other like so many pits in the sea. Fishermen say that if they see they are approaching a whirlpool and have time to throw an oar or some other bulky thing into it, they will get over it safely. The reason is that when the whirling motion of the sea is broken, the water must rush suddenly in on all sides and fill up the cavity.

Among the unusual effects of the tide, perhaps the best known are the bores. Bores exist only in rivers, and are created when for some reason most

The tide withdraws, leaving a stranded crab behind.

Outside the cave, a sea anemone clings to the rock.

fluence over the affairs of sea creatures may be seen all over the world.

The billions upon billions of attached animals, like oysters, mussels, and barnacles, owe their very lives to the sweep of the tides. For the tides bring them the food which they cannot go in search of. These creatures are marvelously adapted to live in the world between the tide lines, a world which is for them a zone of great danger. For they may be dried up or washed away. Enemies can come to them by land and by sea. And their delicate living tissues must somehow withstand the attack of storm waves that can move tons of rock or crack the hardest granite.

But the most remarkable thing about some of these creatures that live between the tides is their time of spawning. It is adapted to fit in with the phases of the moon and the stages of the tide. In Europe the oysters reach the peak of their spawning on the spring tides, which are about two days after the full or the new moon. In the waters of northern Africa there is a sea urchin that releases its eggs into the sea on the nights when the moon is full and, it seems, only then. And in tropical waters in many parts of the world there are small sea worms whose spawning is so perfectly timed in relation to the tides that you can tell just from observing the worms what month it is, what day, and often the time of day as well.

Near Samoa in the Pacific, the palolo worm lives out its life on the bottom of the shallow sea in holes in the rocks and among the masses of corals. Twice each year, during the neap tides of the moon's last quarter in October and November, the worms leave their burrows and rise to the top in swarms that cover the water. For this each worm has broken its body in two—half to remain in the rock tunnel and half to carry the eggs to the surface and there to release them. This happens at dawn on the day before the moon reaches its last quarter, and again on the next day. On the second day of the spawning so many eggs have been spawned that the sea has changed color.

What makes each of these creatures behave like this? Is it the state of the tides that in some mysterious way stimulates them? Or is it some other influence of the moon? It is easier to imagine that it is the pressure and rhythmic movement of the

Carrying in its waves the energy of the tides, a tidal bore moves up against the calm waters of the Petitcodiac River near Moncton, in New Brunswick.

Near the line of high tide where the waves have cast her, a female grunion sticks her head out of the California sand. These fishes respond with an eerie precision to the rhythms of the tide. Their remarkable ways are shown on the following two pages.

123

water that stirs these creatures. But why is it only certain tides of the year that do it? And why is it the fullest tides of the month for some kinds of animals and for others the least? At present no one can answer.

Of all the creatures linked with the tides, the one that has adjusted its life most perfectly to the tidal rhythm is the grunion. This little shimmering fish, about as long as a man's hand, has mysteriously come to know not only the daily rhythm of the tides, but also the fact that certain tides sweep higher on the beaches than others. It does its spawning then—and in a most remarkable fashion. Shortly after the full moon of the months from March to August, the grunion appear in the surf on the beaches of California. The tide reaches flood stage, slackens, hesitates, and begins to ebb. Now on these waves of the ebbing tide the fish begin to come in. Their bodies shimmer in the light of the moon as they are borne up the beach on the crest of a wave. They lie glittering on the wet sand for a moment, then fling themselves into the wash of the next wave and are carried back to sea. For about an hour after the turn of the tide this goes on—thousands upon thousands of grunion come up onto the beach, leave the water, and return to it.

What is the meaning of this?

This is the spawning act of the grunion. During the brief moment between waves, the male and female have come together in the wet sand—the one to shed her eggs, the other to fertilize them. When the fish return to the water, they have left behind a mass of eggs buried in the sand. The waves that follow on that night do not wash out

the eggs because the tide is already ebbing. Nor will the waves of the next high tide reach them, because for a time after the full of the moon each tide halts a little lower on the beach than the one before. The eggs, then, will not be disturbed for at least two weeks. In the warm, damp sand they develop. Within two weeks they have changed from eggs to fishlets. But each fishlet is still confined within the membrane of the egg and is still buried in the sand. It is waiting to be set free. With the tides of the new moon freedom comes. The waves of these stronger tides wash over the places where the little masses of grunion eggs were buried. As the sand is washed away and the eggs feel the touch of the cool sea water, the membranes break. The fishlets hatch. And the waves that set them free carry them away to sea.

Away from the sea, the flatworm remembers the tide.

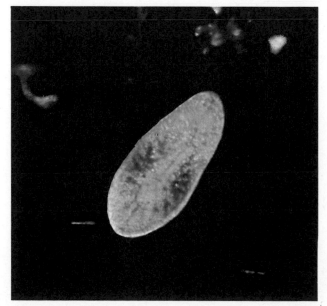

124

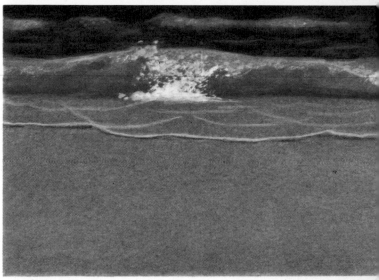

This strange, perfect link with the tides is something to fill us with wonder. But the link I like best to remember is that of a very small flatworm called *Convoluta roscoffensis*. It lives on the sandy beaches of northern Brittany and the Channel Islands. Convoluta has gone into a remarkable partnership with a tiny green seaweed. The worm has taken the seaweed into its own tissues, and the plant gives its green color to them. This worm does not eat. It lives entirely on the starches and sugars manufactured by its plant guest.

Now, to do their work, the plant cells need sunlight. So Convoluta rises from the damp sands as soon as the tide has ebbed, and for the several hours the tide is out, lies in the sun, giving the plants a chance to manufacture their starches and sugars. When the tide returns, the worms must again sink into the sand to avoid being washed out into deep water. So the whole lifetime of the worm is a set of movements that fits in with the tides—up into sunshine on the ebb, down on the flood.

But what I find most unforgettable about Convoluta is this:

Sometimes it happens that a scientist, wishing to study these worms, will transfer a whole colony of them to an aquarium in his laboratory. In the aquarium into which he puts them there are no tides. Yet twice each day Convoluta rises out of the sand on the bottom of the aquarium. And twice each day it sinks back into it. Without a brain, or what we would call a memory, Convoluta continues to live out its life in this unfamiliar place just as it did in the zone between the tides. In some mysterious way it remembers, in every fiber of its small green body, the tidal rhythm of the distant sea.

On moonlit summer nights the grunion invade the California shores. Between the wave that brings them and the wave that carries them away, male and female deposit the fertilized eggs in the sand. In two weeks new fishlets will be carried away to sea.

125

UNITED STATES

Gulf of
Mexico

FLORIDA

GULF ST

Bahama
Islands

ATLANTIC

Cuba

OCEAN

Hispaniola

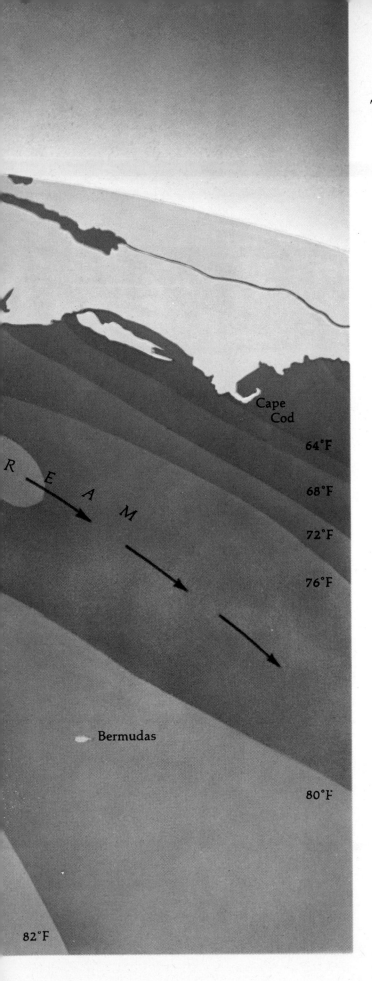

Cape
Cod

64°F

68°F

72°F

76°F

Bermudas

80°F

82°F

The Global Thermostat

WHEN THE building of the Panama Canal was first suggested, many people in Europe criticized the project. The French especially were alarmed.

"Such a canal will allow the waters of the Equatorial Current to escape into the Pacific!" they objected. "Then there will be no Gulf Stream. And that will mean unbearably cold winters for Europe."

The French were completely wrong in their forecast. But they were right in this—they recognized that ocean currents have a great deal to do with climate.

Schemes for changing—or trying to change—the pattern of the currents, and thus changing climate keep coming up from time to time. We hear of projects to divert the cold Oyashio from the coast of Asia. We hear of projects for controlling the Gulf Stream.

About 1912 the Congress of the United States was asked to set aside money to build a jetty from Cape Race eastward across the Grand Banks to shut out the cold water flowing south from the Arctic. Those who were backing the plan believed that the Gulf Stream would then swing in nearer the mainland and would bring warmer winters to the entire east coast, as it does to Florida. The money was not granted. And fortunately so. For even if engineers had succeeded in directing the current, the change would not have had the effect that was expected. Bringing the Gulf Stream nearer would not have made our winters warmer. For our prevailing winds are from the west, and the warm masses of air that have lain over the Gulf Stream seldom reach us anyway. Besides, the nearness of this warm air would have created an area of low pressure—a breeder of stormy weather.

The temperature of the sea changes gradually from place to place. The color bands show July temperature averages of the Atlantic, facing the American coast. They twist sharply at the Gulf Stream.

127

Endless seas of pack ice surround the bleak and windblown regions of the Antarctic.

The Gulf Stream does not affect eastern North America very much. But for the lands lying "downstream" it is vastly different. A branch of the Stream piles up against the coast of Europe the warmest water found so far north anywhere in the world. And as the current rolls up along the Scandinavian coast, many branches curve back westward and bring the breath of warm water to the arctic islands. The west coast of Spitsbergen, warmed by one of these side streams, is bright with flowers in the arctic summer while the east coast remains barren. Passing around the northern tip of Norway, the warm currents keep open such harbors as Hammerfest and Murmansk all through the winter.

The Gulf Stream is always a warm-water current. But its temperature varies from year to year, and even a very slight change makes a difference in the climate of Europe. The North Atlantic has been

compared to "a great bath with a hot tap and two cold taps." The hot tap is the Gulf Stream. The cold taps are the Labrador Current and the East Greenland Current. The cold taps stay nearly the same in temperature and volume, but the hot tap varies. And what the mixture is in any year has a

Flowers bloom on Spitsbergen's Gulf Stream shore.

128

great deal to do with what happens in Europe and the arctic seas. When the Gulf Stream is a little warmer, it means that the snow will melt earlier in Europe, the spring plowing may begin sooner, the harvest will be better. It means, too, that there will be less ice near Iceland in the spring and that a year or two later the drift ice in the Barents Sea will diminish.

For the globe as a whole, the ocean is the great heat regulator. As someone has said, it is a sort of savings bank for the heat of the sun. It receives deposits when there is too much heat from the sun and pays them back in seasons when there is not enough. By distributing heat and cold over thousands of miles, the ocean currents make up for the fact that the sun heats the globe unevenly. In this work the winds also take part. About half is done by the currents and half by the winds.

The ocean of water and the ocean of air that lies over it work very closely together in shifting the heat around. And they have a great influence on each other.

The atmosphere warms or cools the ocean and receives its vapors through evaporation. As the weight of the air changes and the atmosphere bears down on the ocean more here and less there, the ocean dips down in one place and springs up in another. The winds—which are air in motion—grip the surface of the sea and raise it into waves. They drive the currents onward.

The ocean affects the air even more. The air transfers a little heat to the sea. But the sea transfers a great deal more heat to the air. For it is much easier to heat air than to heat water. In fact, it is 3000 times easier.

Now the temperature of the air has a great deal to do with its weight—the colder the air, the heavier it is. Where the air is cold, pressure tends to be high, where the air is warm, it tends to be low. So when the ocean passes heat on to the air, it changes the various areas of high and low pressure. And this greatly affects the winds. It determines their force and direction. It directs the storms on their paths.

By evaporation, the ocean also transfers moisture to the air. Most of the rains that fall, on sea and land alike, were raised from the sea. In the United States, vapor and warm air from the Gulf of Mexico and the tropical waters of the western Atlantic ride the winds up the wide valley of the Mississippi and provide rain for the eastern part of North America.

The rich store of minerals in its waters enables the Arctic to support a great variety of life.

No land mammal could survive on the Antarctic ice, but a few hardy creatures brave the surrounding seas. An old seal here lies on the ice off McMurdo Sound; in the distance is Mount Erebus.

Nearness to the sea, as a general thing, has a moderating effect on climate. But the pattern of the currents, and of winds, and of mountains decides how great that effect shall be. The east coast of North America, for instance, gets little benefit from the sea because the prevailing winds are from the west. The Pacific coast, on the other hand, is fortunate. It lies in the path of the westerly winds that have blown across thousands of miles of ocean. The moist breath of the Pacific softens the climate. It also creates the dense rain forests of British Columbia, Washington, and Oregon. However, only a narrow strip along the edge of the continent gets the full effect of the sea—for the coast ranges stand in the way. By contrast, Europe lies wide open to the influence of the ocean, for it has no coastal range. So "Atlantic weather" goes hundreds of miles in.

The sea transforms climate. And how completely it does so is strikingly seen in the differences between the Arctic and the Antarctic.

The Arctic is a sea almost closed in by land; the Antarctic is a continent surrounded by ocean. The ice-covered Antarctic is in the grip of high winds that blow outward from the land. They ward off any warming influence that might otherwise come to the continent from the sea. So the Antarctic is a bitterly cold land. On exposed rocks, lichens grow. Here and there over the snow is the red dust of very small and simple plant cells. Mosses hide from the wind in the valleys and crevices. But of the higher plants only a few skimpy stands of grasses have managed to find a foothold. There are no land mammals. The animals of the Antarctic continent are birds, a wingless mosquito, a few flies, and a microscopic mite.

Contrast with this the summers of the Arctic! Its flat, treeless plains are bright with many-colored flowers. Everywhere except on the Greenland ice-cap and some arctic islands, summer is warm enough for plants to grow. They pack a year's growth into the short, warm, arctic summer. The

Nourished by water from melting ice, mountain flowers bloom in the brief arctic summer.

limit of plant life toward the poles is set not by latitude, but by the sea. For the influence of the warm Atlantic is borne far up into the Arctic, making it in climate as well as geography a world apart from the Antarctic.

So, day by day and season by season, the ocean dominates the world's climate. What about the long-period swings? Does the ocean have anything to do with them? Does it play any part in bringing about the periods of heat and cold that have come and gone through the long history of the earth?

There is a fascinating theory that it does. This theory links what happens in the deep, hidden places of the ocean with the great swings of climate and their effects on human history. The theory was set forth by the Swedish scientist Otto Pettersson. Pettersson's work was perhaps a natural result of the circumstances of his life. He was born—as he died 93 years later—on the shores of the Baltic. In his laboratory atop a sheer cliff overlooking the deep waters of the Gulmarfiord, instruments recorded strange happenings in the

Lichens grow in both polar regions, but only in the Arctic are they as large and bright as these.

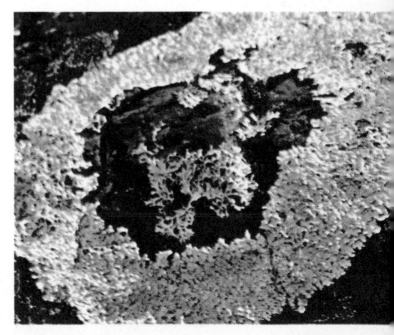

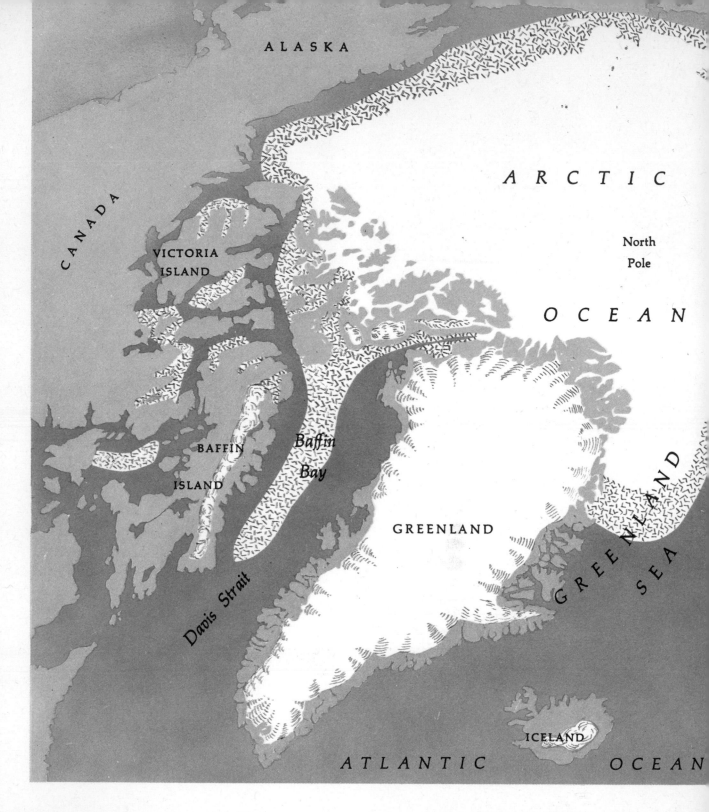

ALASKA

CANADA

VICTORIA
ISLAND

BAFFIN

ISLAND

Baffin

Bay

Davis Strait

ARCTIC

North
Pole

OCEAN

GREENLAND

GREENLAND

SEA

ICELAND

ATLANTIC   OCEAN

depths of this gateway to the Baltic. As the
ocean water presses in toward that inland sea it
dips down and lets the fresh surface water roll out
above it; and at that deep level where salt and
fresh water come into contact there is a layer where
the change is very sharp, like the surface film between water and air. Each day Pettersson's instruments revealed a strong, pulsing movement of that

deep layer—the pressing inward of great submarine
waves, of moving mountains of water. The movement was strongest every twelfth hour of the day,
and between the 12-hour intervals it grew weaker.
Pettersson soon established a link between these
submarine waves and the daily tides. "Moon
waves," he called them. As he measured their
height and timed their pulsing beat through the

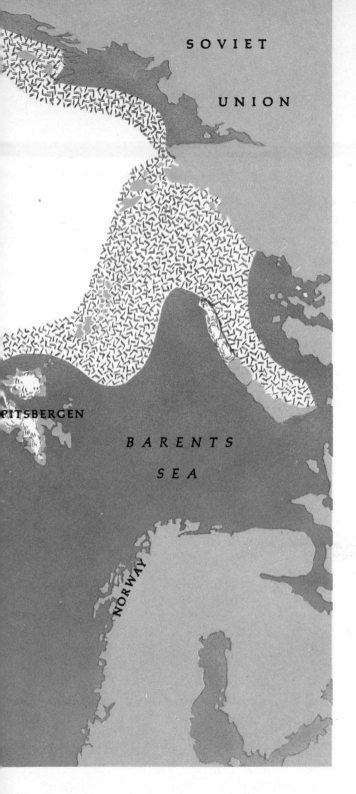

SOVIET

UNION

SPITSBERGEN

BARENTS

SEA

NORWAY

weakest tides were about A.D. 550 and will come again about the year 2400.

During the latest period of mild climate, snow and ice were little known on the coast of Europe and in the seas about Iceland and Greenland. Then the Vikings sailed freely over northern seas. The early Norse writings tell of the abundant fruit of excellent quality that grew then in Greenland, and of the number of cattle that could be pastured there. The Norwegian settlements were located then in places that are now at the foot of glaciers.

But in the thirteenth century the climate began to worsen. It was at that time that the Eskimos began to make troublesome raids. It seems likely that they did so because their northern sealing grounds were frozen over and they were hungry. The Norse settlements in Greenland were wiped out.

Europe at this time was also feeling the change in climate. Holland was devastated by storm floods. Packs of wolves crossed on the ice from Norway to Denmark. The entire Baltic froze over so that there was a bridge of solid ice between Sweden and Denmark. Travelers crossed the frozen sea in carriages and on foot and hostelries were put up on the ice to accommodate them. In southern Europe there were unusual storms, crop failures, and famine.

Now, according to Pettersson's tidal theory, there should also have been an era of cold and storms about the third or fourth century B.C. Does that check with history?

It seems that it does. There are hints of it in early writings and in folklore. The early Norse writings tell of a great disaster, a period when frost and snow ruled the world for generations. Early history suggests that the "barbarians" who shook the power of Rome were forced south because of storms and floods. There were floods in Jutland, whole tribes were driven out of their homelands by the ocean, trade routes had to be shifted.

All these records of changes in climate seemed to Pettersson to show that the circulation of the ocean had been upset. He believed that the changes in climate were brought about when submarine tidal waves disturbed the deep waters of polar seas. In these seas the surface tides are usually weak. But

months and years, their relation to the ever-changing cycles of the tides became crystal clear.

Pettersson published his theory of changing climates in 1912. He suggested that the alternating periods of mild and severe climates are caused by regular changes in the deep ocean tides. The most recent period of strongest tides and coldest climate was, he said, about the year 1433. The world's

133

In some years, great numbers of icebergs break off from the ice shelves bordering Greenland. Drifting down on the Labrador Current, their gigantic hulks come sailing into the Atlantic.

they set up strong submarine waves. In the years when the tides are strong, great quantities of warm Atlantic water press into the Arctic Sea. They move in deep under the ice. Then thousands of square miles of ice that usually stay frozen break up. Drift ice in great quantities enters the Labrador Current and is carried southward into the Atlantic. The drift ice attacks the Gulf Stream and turns it more to the east. Then the warm streams that usually soften the climate of Greenland, Iceland, Spitsbergen, and northern Europe do not penetrate far north.

According to Pettersson, the really strong disturbances come only every 18 centuries. At these times, sun, moon and earth come into a particular position in relation to each other that makes the tidal force the strongest possible. But in between there are shorter swings of climate. These, he worked out, come every 9, 18, or 36 years.

The year 1903, for instance, was a memorable year for polar ice in the Arctic and the effect of that ice on Scandinavian fisheries. There was a general failure of cod, herring, and other fish. The year 1912—nine years later—was another great ice year in the Labrador Current. And that was the year that brought the disaster of the *Titanic*.

Now in our own lifetime we are seeing a startling change of climate, and it is tempting to apply Otto

Pettersson's ideas as an explanation. It is now established beyond question that a definite change in the arctic climate set in about 1900. It became astonishingly marked about 1930, and at present it is spreading into sub-arctic and temperate regions. The icy top of the world is very clearly warming up.

We see it best of all in the fact that navigation is easier in the North Atlantic and the Arctic Sea. In 1932, for example, a vessel sailed around Franz Josef Land, an island in the very high Arctic, for the first time in history. And three years later a Russian icebreaker reached 82° 41′ north latitude—which is as far north as a ship ever got under its own power.

In the summer of 1940, the whole northern coast of Europe and Asia was remarkably free from ice. Then more than 100 ships made trade voyages by the arctic routes. In 1942 a ship unloaded supplies at a port in latitude 72° 43′ during Christmas week in almost complete winter darkness. During the forties, the season when pack ice lies about Iceland became shorter by about two months than it was a hundred years ago. Drift ice in the Russian part of the Arctic Sea decreased by 400,000 square miles between 1924 and 1944.

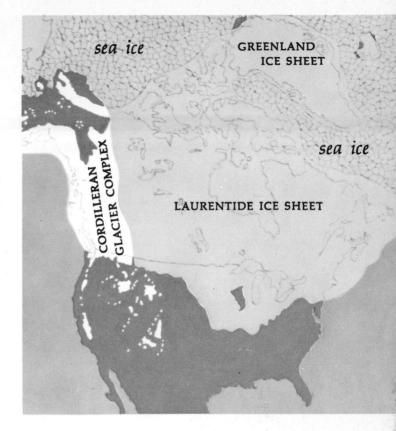

The most recent ice age may have occurred only ten thousand years ago—well within the time of man. Ice sheets then covered vast areas of North America.

Endless stretches of drift ice rim the western shores of Greenland.

With the warming up of the Arctic, birds of temperate regions have recently been seen in Greenland.

BLACK-BROWED ALBATROSS

COMMON CROSSBILL

OVENBIRD

VELVET SCOTER

What is happening in the animal world also shows us that the Arctic is warming up. Many fishes, birds, land mammals, and whales have changed their habits and migrations.

New birds are appearing in far northern lands for the first time to our knowledge. The velvet scoter now comes to Greenland. So also do the greater yellowlegs, the American avocet, the black-browed albatross, the northern cliff swallow, the ovenbird, the common crossbill, the Baltimore oriole, and Canada warbler. On the other hand, some arctic birds show their dislike of the warmer weather by coming to Greenland less and less.

Then there is the cod. When cod first appeared at Angmagssalik on the east coast of Greenland in 1912, it was a new and strange fish to the Eskimos and Danes. They began to catch it, and by the 1930's had not only become dependent on it for food, but were using its oil as fuel for their lamps and to heat their houses.

Other fishes seldom or never before reported in Greenland have appeared there. When two green cod were caught in 1831, they seemed so curious

CANADA WARBLER

AMERICAN AVOCET

GREATER YELLOWLEGS

NORTHERN CLIFF SWALLOW

BALTIMORE ORIOLE

that they were promptly preserved and sent to the Copenhagen Zoological Museum. Now they are often taken. And the haddock, cusk, and ling, unknown in Greenland waters until about 1930, are caught regularly. Iceland, too, has strange visitors —warmth-loving southern fishes like the basking shark, the sunfish, the swordfish, and the horse mackerel. Some of these have even gone up into the Barents and the White Seas.

On every hand there is evidence that the top of the world is growing warmer. The northern glaciers are going so fast that many smaller ones have disappeared already, and if melting keeps on at the same rate, others will soon follow them.

In Norway the melting away of the snowfields has brought to light arrows of a type used about A.D. 400 to 500. This means that the snow cover in that region is less than any time in the last 1400 to 1500 years. Reports say that most glaciers in Norway are getting no fresh supplies of snow. In the Alps and around the Northern Atlantic coasts all the glaciers are shrinking. The fastest melting is going on in Alaska, where the Muir Glacier has retreated about 6½ miles in 12 years.

At present less is known about the rate at which the vast antarctic glaciers may be melting. But the glaciers of several high East African volcanoes have been very rapidly shrinking since 1920. And so have glaciers in the Andes and the high mountains of central Asia.

It is almost certainly true that over the next thousand years the world's climate will grow considerably warmer, for we are in the warming-up stage after the last glacial period. The swing back into another Ice Age is still far off. But what we

are having now is something apart from the long-period swing. It may be only a short-run change of climate within the upward swing toward warmer weather.

Some scientists say the sun is responsible. They say it is giving out more heat. Over against that we have Pettersson's tidal theory.

If it is right, then it is interesting to work out where we are in the warming up. The great tides with their accompanying snow and ice, their furious winds and floods, are more than five centuries behind us. The period of weakest tides is about four centuries ahead. We have therefore begun to move strongly into a period of warmer, milder weather. There will·be ups and downs as the power of the tides waxes and wanes. But the long trend is toward a warmer earth. The pendulum is swinging.

A native bird of the very far north, the eider duck builds its nest from down plucked from its breast. The nest is sheltered by a circular hedge of alpine foxtail that has taken root and sprouted around it.

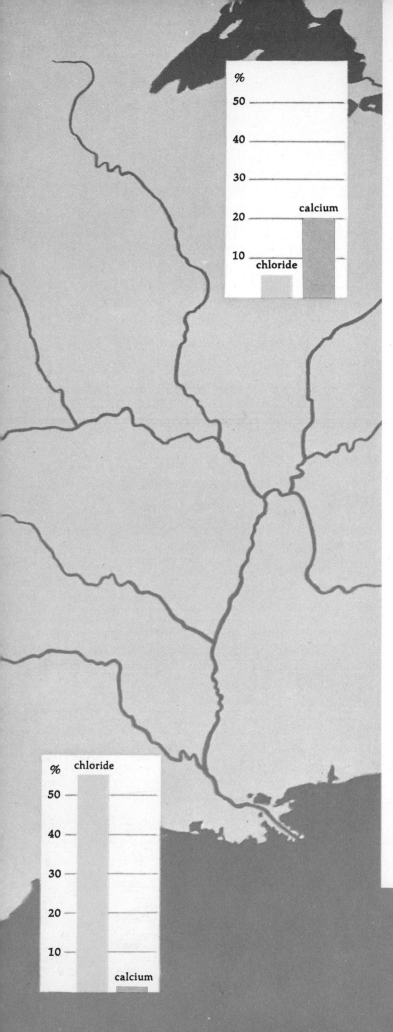

%
50 ——————
40 ——————
30 ——————
calcium
20 ——————
10 ——————
chloride

% chloride
50 —
40 —
30 —
20 —
10 —
calcium

When river water reaches the sea it undergoes great changes. Some things in it—salt, especially—keep on accumulating in the water; others, like calcium, drop to the bottom, as sediments, or are taken up by millions of sea creatures to become shells.

Wealth from the Salt Seas

THE OCEAN is the earth's greatest storehouse of minerals. In a single cubic mile of sea water there are, on the average, 166 million tons of dissolved salts, and in all the ocean waters of the earth there are about 50 quadrillion tons.

Where has it all come from?

We have to suppose that the first seas were only faintly salt. They have been getting saltier over the eons of time and will gradually get even more salty. For the rocks of the continents are the great source of the ocean's salt. When the first rains came—those centuries-long rains that fell from the heavy clouds which enveloped the young earth —they began to wear away the rocks and carry minerals to the sea. Every year since then several billion tons of salts have been added to the sea.

Now it is a curious fact that river and sea water are very different—the chemicals in them are present in entirely different proportions. The rivers bring into the sea four times as much calcium as chloride, for example. Yet it is astonishing to find that the ocean has 46 times as much chloride as calcium. How can this be?

Part of the answer is that the animals of the sea take out immense amounts of calcium salts to build their shells and skeletons. For all the tiny shells that house the small creatures known as foraminifera, for all the coral reefs, for all the shells of oysters and clams and other mollusks, calcium is drawn out of the sea. Another reason is precipitation—some of the dissolved calcium that the rivers bring into the sea turns back into solids and becomes limestone. There is a striking difference in the amount of silica in river and in sea water, too. River water contains 500 times more silica. For in the sea the silica is taken up by diatoms to make their shells.

Not all the minerals are borne into the sea by streams. From every volcano chlorine and other gases escape into the air. These are carried down on the surface of the sea as well as on the land. Volcanic ash and rock bring up other materials. And all the hidden submarine volcanoes pour boron, chlorine, sulfur, and iodine directly into the sea.

All this is a one-way flow—very little gets back to the land. We try to recover some of the chemicals by various processes. We also harvest the sea's plants and animals. And, of course, when the seas overflow the lands, deposit sediments, and at last withdraw, they leave some of the salts behind. But this is only a temporary loan. For the return payment begins at once. The rains dissolve the minerals, erosion breaks the rocks into fragments, and the rivers carry all back to the sea again.

There are other curious little exchanges between sea and land. When evaporation takes place, most of the salts are left behind. But a surprising amount of salt does get into the air and rides long distances on the wind. This is salt that is picked up by the winds from the spray of a rough sea or from breaking surf. It is blown inland and is then brought down in rain. England gets 24 to 36 pounds of this traveling salt per acre per year. British Guiana gets 100 pounds. But the place that gets most is Sambhar Salt Lake in northern India. This lake receives 3000 tons of this air-borne salt a year. It is carried on the hot, dry summer winds from the sea, 400 miles away.

Taking the calcium from the sea, clams fashion it into the hard shells that will be their protection.

Long before chemists had given vanadium a thought, the sea cucumber had concentrated it in its blood.

The plants and animals of the sea are much better chemists than we are. They are able to find chemicals of which there is just a trace in sea water. Vanadium, for instance, is a metal that has been in use for several generations; but we did not know that there was vanadium in the sea until it was discovered in the blood of a group of sluggish sea creatures, including the sea cucumber. Lobsters and mussels extract huge quantities of cobalt. Various mollusks make use of nickel. Lobsters draw out copper, which becomes part of their blood—the way iron forms part of human blood.

Of all the elements present in the sea, probably none has stirred men's dreams more than gold. It is there—indeed, in all the waters over the earth there is enough gold to make every person in the world a millionaire. But how can the sea be made to yield it?

After the First World War a German chemist conceived the idea of extracting enough gold from the sea to pay the German war debt. His dream resulted in the German South Atlantic Expedition of the *Meteor*. The *Meteor* was equipped with a laboratory and between the years 1924 and 1928 the vessel crossed and recrossed the Atlantic, sampling the water. But the amount was found to be less than expected—that is, in a cubic mile of sea water there is about $93,000,000 in gold; but to treat this volume of water in a year the ship would have had to process so many tankfuls of water per day, and at such a tremendous cost, that it was not worth doing.

Most mysterious, perhaps, of all substances in the sea is iodine. In the sea water itself it is difficult to detect. Yet it is found in almost every sea plant and animal. Sponges, corals, and certain seaweeds have vast quantities of it. We ourselves could not exist without the iodine that is gathered by a gland near our Adam's apple—the thyroid.

As they lead their lives by the world's shores, lobsters and mussels extract cobalt from the ocean.

140

Murex was the snail the Phoenicians used to make Tyrian purple, a bromine dye. Deposits of billions of snails, in the hot springs under the Sea of Galilee, may be the source of the bromine that the River Jordan has been carrying south into the Dead Sea.

All commercial iodine used to be extracted from seaweeds. Later, deposits of crude nitrate of soda were discovered in the high deserts of Chile, where probably they were left by some prehistoric sea filled with marine plants. Iodine is obtained, too, from brine deposits and from oil-bearing rocks— which once were under the sea.

Of bromine, the ocean has the world's monopoly—99 per cent. There are large plants on the seacoasts—especially in our country—for getting the bromine out of ocean water. For bromine goes into high-test gasoline It is used also for making drugs with a calming effect, and in fire extinguishers, photographic chemicals, and dyestuffs.

One of the oldest things derived from bromine was Tyrian purple. This was a wonderful dye which the Phoenicians made at great expense from the purple snail Murex. Tyrian purple was so highly prized, especially by kings, that it enabled the Phoenicians to become the greatest traders of their age. Perhaps this little snail is responsible for the amazing quantities of bromine in the Dead Sea, which are estimated to be some 850 million tons. In the water of that sea there is a hundred times as much bromine as in ocean water. Apparently the supply is constantly renewed by underground hot springs which discharge into the Sea of Galilee and are carried by the River Jordan to the Dead Sea. Some scientists believe that the bromine of the hot springs comes from a deposit of billions of ancient snails, laid down by the sea of a bygone age.

Magnesium is another mineral we now get from the sea. There are about 4 million tons of magnesium to a cubic mile of sea water. About half a ton of magnesium metal goes into every airplane made in the United States. It has countless other uses, too, where a light-weight metal is wanted. Besides this, it is used in printing inks, medicines, toothpastes, and in incendiary bombs, star shells, and tracer ammunition.

Almost every plant or animal of the sea contains iodine—kelp long was a commercial source of it.

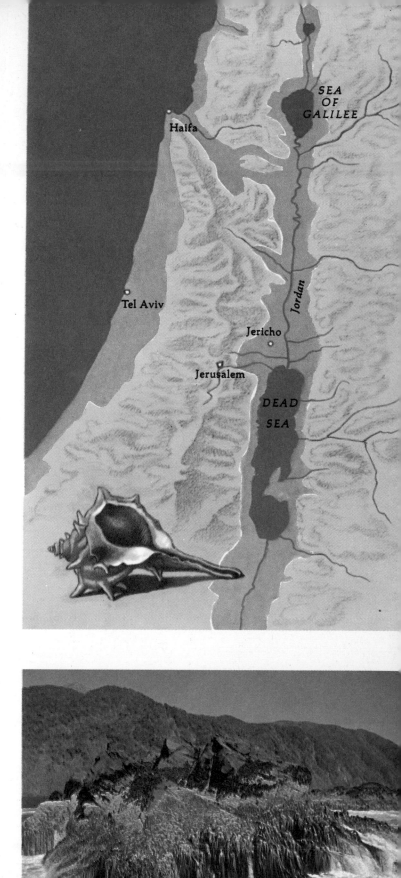

When Hernando Cortes navigated it during his conquest of Mexico, Lake Texcoco was twelve miles long. In later years it shrank greatly, showering nearby Mexico City with salt dust. This spiral evaporation pool lets the lake salt condense so that it can be harvested.

As we would expect, sodium chloride—common salt—is the most abundant of the salts in the ocean. And wherever climate has permitted it, men have for centuries evaporated sea water to get this salt—which all men and animals must have in order to live. Even today, in parts of the world that are hot and dry and where drying winds blow, this is the way people get salt.

Here and there in natural basins the sun and wind of their own accord do the same job on a scale that man could not hope to achieve. The Rann of Cutch is such a basin on the west coast of India. The Rann is a flat plain, some 60 by 185 miles—almost the size of Lake Michigan. It is separated from the sea by the island of Cutch. When the southwest winds blow, sea water is carried in to cover the plain. But in summer the hot wind

blows from the desert the other way. No more water comes in. The water that has collected over the plain evaporates into a salt crust which in some places is several feet thick.

In Europe and the United States it is not necessary to evaporate sea water to get salt. For ancient seas have made the task much easier. They have left deposits of common salt, and other salts, too. Two hundred million years ago a vast inland sea overran much of Europe. It covered Britain, France, Germany, and Poland. Now this was a period of great heat and dryness. Since evaporation was high and little rain came in, the inland sea became very salty and began to deposit layers of salts. For thousands of years only gypsum was deposited. This gypsum alternated with thicker beds of salt. Later, other salts were laid down.

After the sea had completely evaporated, the salts were all buried under sand. The richest of these beds of chemicals form the famous Stassfurt deposits in Germany. These beds are about 2500 feet thick.

Still earlier—about 350 million years ago—a great salt basin was deposited in the northern part of the United States. It stretched from central New York State across Michigan, northern Pennsylvania and Ohio, and part of southern Ontario. The climate was hot and dry at that time, too, and the inland sea grew very salty. Beds of salt and gypsum were deposited over an area covering 100,000 square miles. At Ithaca, New York, there are seven distinct beds of salt, the uppermost lying half a mile down. In southern Michigan, some of the individual salt beds are more than 500 feet thick. In the Michigan Basin the total thickness is 2000 feet. In some places the rock salt is mined directly. In others, wells are dug and water is forced down to make brine. Then the brine is pumped up and evaporated to get the salt.

One of the greatest stockpiles of minerals in the world was laid up by a lost inland sea in western United States. This is Searles Lake in the Mojave

Rows of spray pipes stand among the piles of condensed Glauber's salt in Searles Lake in California.

Desert of California. An arm of the sea was cut off when a range of mountains rose. As the lake evaporated, the water became ever more salty from the inwash of minerals from all the land around. At last all the water vanished, leaving behind a "frozen" lake—a lake of solid minerals—over which a car may be driven. The salts are 50 to 70 feet deep. Below that is mud, and under the mud is a second layer of salts and brine. Searles Lake was first worked for borax. In the 1800's teams of

Spanning the vast area once covered by an inland sea, a road cuts across the mineral beds of Searles Lake.

Amid the dunes in the Arabian sands, petroleum wells up from sediments left by seas of a distant past.

20 mules each carried the borax across desert and mountains to the railroads. In the 1930's other substances began to be recovered from the lake. Now Searles Lake yields two-fifths of all the potassium chloride produced in the United States and a large share of the borax and lithium salts produced in the world.

Some day the Dead Sea will probably repeat the history of Searles Lake. Once this sea was four times as large. It is shrinking and shrinking in the hot, dry climate, and all the more because its waters are warmer than the air. The Dead Sea is so heavy with salts now that no animal can live in it. Such unlucky fish as are brought down by the River Jordan die and provide food for the sea birds. It is 1300 feet below the Mediterranean and lies farther below sea level than any other body of water in the world.

The ancient seas have left behind many valuable things, but of them all the most valuable is petroleum. Exactly how these precious pools deep in the earth were made, no one knows in detail. Scientists used to believe that petroleum was made by volcanic action. Today most of them believe that it comes from living things—from plants and animals buried under the fine sediments of former seas, where they have slowly decomposed.

The Black Sea is a good example of the conditions under which this can happen. There is a great deal of life in the upper layers of the Black Sea. But lower down no creatures can exist because there is no oxygen in the bottom waters and because hydrogen sulfide often poisons them. So there are no scavengers to eat up the bodies of dead creatures that drift down from above. Whatever drifts down is buried in the fine sediments.

144

Wherever great oil fields are found, they are related to past or present seas. The great quantities of oil that have been taken from the Oklahoma fields, for instance, were trapped in the empty spaces of rocks laid down under seas that invaded this part of North America between 200 and 400 million years ago. The vast oil deposits of Saudi Arabia, Iran, and Iraq are in areas that have lain sometimes under the sea and sometimes above it. A shallow, island-studded sea lies between the continents of Asia and Australia. This area, too, has been lifted up and lowered time and again, and in this area we have the oil of Java, Sumatra, Borneo, and New Guinea.

In recent years petroleum geologists have been turning their eyes in a new direction—undersea. For although not all the oil resources on land have been found, probably the richest fields and the ones easiest to work are being tapped. Can the ocean be made to give up some of the oil that must be trapped in rocks under its floor?

Oil is already being taken out of wells on the continental shelf off California, Texas, and Louisiana. The Gulf of Mexico offers much promise. For it was for ages either dry land or a very shallow sea. Sediments were washed into this shallow sea from the high lands to the north. And finally about 60 million years ago the floor sank under the load and got its present deep basin.

So our search for mineral wealth often leads us back to the seas of ancient times. We search for the oil pressed from the bodies of fishes, seaweeds, and other forms of plant and animal life. We use the rich brines hidden in pools under the earth. We mine the layers of salts which those old seas laid down as a covering mantle over the continents.

Perhaps in time we shall learn the chemical secrets of the corals and diatoms. Then we shall depend less on the wealth which the prehistoric seas have stored. We shall go more and more directly to the ocean and the rocks now forming under its shallow waters.

Beyond the land, vast reserves of petroleum lie under the shallow waters off the continental shelves.

The more distant the sea, the more it seemed filled with monsters.

The Encircling Sea

To THE ancient Greeks the ocean was an endless stream that flowed forever around the border of the world. This ocean was boundless. If a person were to venture far out upon it, he would pass through gathering darkness and fog and would come at last to a dreadful region where sea and sky came together. There he would find himself among whirlpools and yawning abysses that waited to draw him down into a dark world from which there was no return.

With variations, these ideas appear over and over again in ancient writings for a thousand years before the birth of Christ. To the Greeks the familiar Mediterranean was The Sea. It was all the sea there was except for Oceanus, washing around the edge of the world. As to exactly what lay at the uttermost limits of Oceanus, the Greeks were a little confused. Somewhere off there, they believed, were the Elysian fields, a happy land where there was neither snow, nor cold, nor rain, a land to which favored heroes passed without dying. Some spoke of continents and beautiful islands in that distant ocean. Others made mention of a bottomless gulf at the very edge. But always in

146

every description, around the disc of the habitable world was the vast ocean, encircling all.

Some of the ideas of what lay at the edge of the world may have been suggested to the Greeks by the eye-witness accounts of traders who went north for amber and tin. They must have brought back a picture of fog and storms and darkness. So poets wrote of Cimmerians dwelling in a distant realm of mist and darkness on the shores of Oceanus. They wrote of shepherds who lived in the land of the long day, where only a few hours separated the setting and the rising of the sun.

And again, perhaps the early writers got some of their ideas of the ocean from the Phoenicians, whose craft roamed the shores of Europe, Asia, and Africa in search of gold, silver, gems, spices, and wood. It may well be that these sailor-merchants were the first ever to cross an ocean. History says nothing of that. But it is certain that for at least 2000 years before Christ these bold sailors carried their trade along the shores of the Red Sea to Syria, to Somaliland, to Arabia, even to India and perhaps China. The Phoenicians wrote little about their voyagings—they wanted to keep their trade routes and the places where they got their cargoes secret. So they may, or may not, have launched out into the open Pacific.

Did the Phoenicians get north as far as the Baltic, source of the precious amber? Perhaps. There is an account of the voyage of one Himlico of Carthage who sailed northward along the European coast about the year 500 B.C. His own manuscript was not preserved, but his descriptions were quoted in later writings. Himlico did not paint an inspiring picture of the coastwise seas of Europe.

These seas can scarcely be sailed through in four months, he is quoted as saying. *No breeze drives the ship forward, so dead is the sluggish wind of this idle sea . . . There is much seaweed among the waves . . . the surface of the earth is barely covered by a little water . . . The monsters of the sea move continually hither and thither, and the wild beasts swim among the sluggish and slowly creeping ships.*

Perhaps the "wild beasts" were the whales of the Bay of Biscay, bounded by France and Spain, which later became a famous whaling ground. The shallow water areas that so impressed Himlico

The "very terrible sea animal" seen in 1734 to the west of Greenland by the Reverend Hans Egede.

may have been the flats of the French coast, exposed by the ebb of the tide. They must have appeared strange to him, coming from the Mediterranean, which has almost no tide.

Himlico seems also to have had some ideas about a boundless ocean out to the west, beyond the Straits of Gibraltar, whose rocky sides were known in his day as the Pillars of Hercules. "None has sailed ships over these waters," he said, "because propelling winds are lacking on these deeps . . . likewise because darkness screens the light of day with a sort of clothing, and because fog always conceals the sea."

Held in affectionate regard by the inhabitants of the Greek islands, the creatures of the Aegean Sea sometimes turned up on coins, as did this octopus.

147

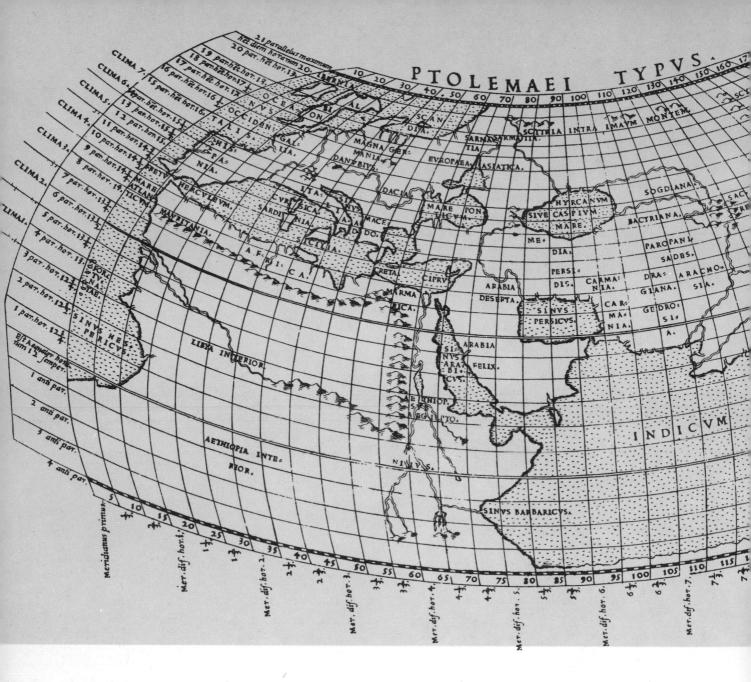

Perhaps the mariner was just painting a dark picture on purpose. Maybe he wanted to discourage others from seeking his trade routes. Or perhaps these notions are just the same old ideas about the Atlantic that everybody had had for ages and that would keep echoing down the centuries to the very threshold of modern times.

Everything about Himlico and his journey is a "perhaps." And not much more can be said about Pytheas of Massilia—the old Roman name for Marseilles—who about 330 B.C. made the first great voyage to explore the sea. He went northward, probably to see how far the land world stretched, and to see the land of the midnight sun,

of which traders had brought tales. He seems to have sailed around Great Britain, reached the Shetland Islands, and then launched out into the open ocean, coming at last to "Thule," the land of the midnight sun. "In this country," he is quoted as reporting, "the nights were very short, in some places two, in others three hours long, so that the sun rose again a short time after it had set."

"Barbarians" showed Pytheas "the place where the sun goes to rest." Was this country Iceland? Or was it Norway? The fact that Pytheas described a "congealed sea" would lead us to believe it was Iceland.

148

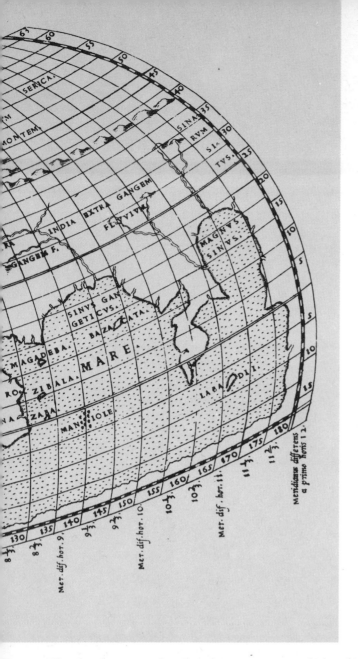

*When the navigators of the great age of discovery
set out to explore unknown seas, their picture of the
world was close to the one given in this map, which
appeared in a Venetian geography of 1561. It was
derived, through a long tradition, from Ptolemy, a
scholar and astronomer of the second century A.D.*

Soon after this exploit, the Dark Ages settled
on the civilized world, and little of the knowledge
acquired by Pytheas seems to have impressed the
men who followed him. The geographer Posidonius sailed from Rhodes all the way to the Atlantic
port of Cadiz to find out whether the sun really
dropped with a hiss into the great western sea.

Not for about 1200 years after Pytheas do we
have another clear account of exploration by sea—
this time by the Norwegian Ottar. Ottar went to
visit King Alfred of England and also sailed up into
the Barents Sea and the White Sea. It seems he
went there "chiefly to explore the country, and for
the sake of the walrus, for they have much valuable
bone in their tusks." This was probably beetween
the years 870 and 890.

Meanwhile the age of the Vikings had dawned.
The Norwegian explorer Fridtjof Nansen has
written of the Vikings' struggle with ice, storms,
cold, and want. "They had," he notes, "neither
compass, nor astronomical instruments, nor any
of the appliances of our time for finding their
position at sea; they could only sail by the sun,
moon, and stars, and it seems incomprehensible
how for days and weeks, when these were invisible,

The Greek geographer Posidonius once traveled to the Atlantic to hear the sun drop with a hiss into the sea.

they were able to find their course through fog and bad weather; but they found it, and in the open craft of the Norwegian Vikings, with their square sails, fared north and west over the whole ocean, from Novaya Zemlya and Spitsbergen to Greenland, Baffin Bay, Newfoundland, and North America. . . ."

But of all this only the vaguest rumors reached the "civilized world" of the Mediterranean. While the Norsemen were writing clear directions how to cross oceans from known to unknown worlds, European scholars were still writing about the dread Sea of Darkness that encircled the world. And even when Columbus and his men set out, there still hung over the Western Ocean the legend of a dead and stagnant sea, of monsters and entrapping weeds, of fog and gloom, and ever-present danger.

Yet centuries before Columbus—how many no one knows—men on the opposite side of the world were boldly sailing their craft across the Pacific.

Through sheer seamanship and without instruments, the Vikings sailed from the islands north of Russia to Newfoundland and North American shores.

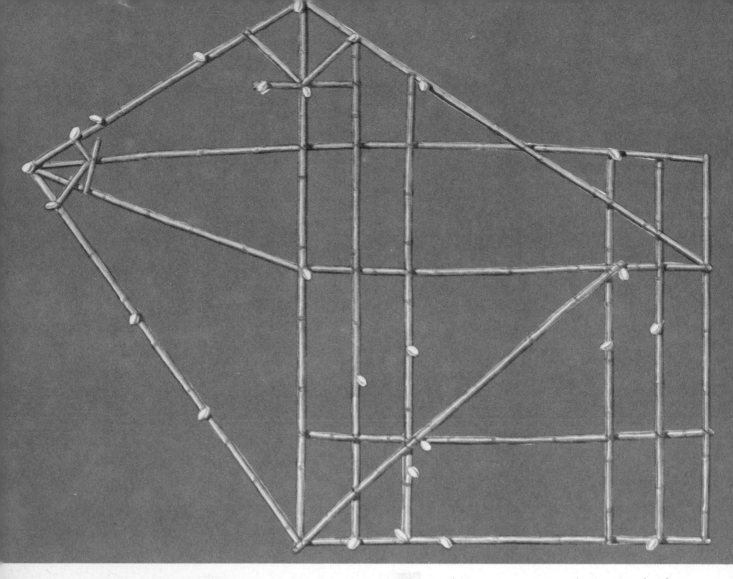

Shell-studded rattan charts guided the Marshall Islanders in their voyages among the Pacific islands.

Perhaps the Pacific seemed a kindlier ocean—it probably did. For these men, the Polynesians, entrusted themselves to it in their open canoes. They had only the stars to guide them, but they found their way from island to island and colonized them.

We do not know when the first of these voyages took place. The last important one to the Hawaiian Islands was made in the thirteenth century. About a hundred years later a fleet from Tahiti colonized New Zealand. But again, all these things were unknown in Europe. And long after the Polynesians had mastered the art of navigating the unknown seas that surrounded them, the European sailors still regarded the Pillars of Hercules as the gateway to a dreaded Sea of Darkness.

Once Columbus had shown the way to the West Indies and the Americas, once Balboa had seen

the Pacific and Magellan had sailed around the globe, the ocean began to lose its terrors. Little by little, through many voyages undertaken over many centuries, the fog and frightening dimness of the unknown were lifted from all the surface of the Sea of Darkness.

How did they accomplish it—those first voyagers? They had not even the simplest instruments of navigation. They had never seen a nautical chart. To them the modern miracles of loran, radar, and sonic sounding would have been fantasies beyond belief. Which of them was the first to use a mariner's compass? And what were the first charts and the first sailing directions like? Of all this we know only enough to want to know more.

We cannot even guess how those secretive

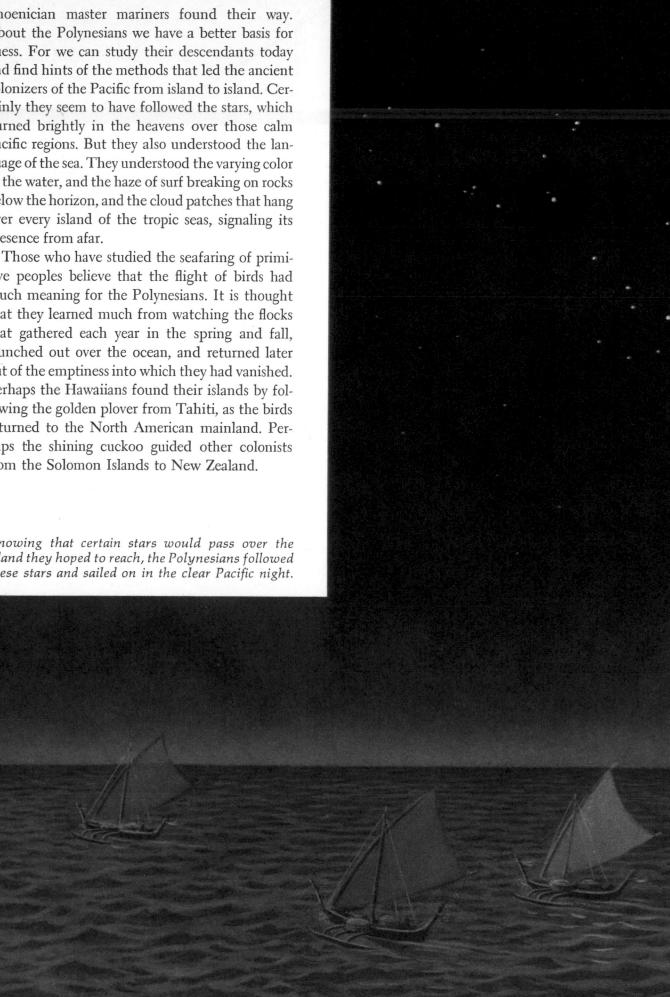

Phoenician master mariners found their way.
About the Polynesians we have a better basis for
guess. For we can study their descendants today
and find hints of the methods that led the ancient
colonizers of the Pacific from island to island. Certainly they seem to have followed the stars, which
burned brightly in the heavens over those calm
Pacific regions. But they also understood the language of the sea. They understood the varying color
of the water, and the haze of surf breaking on rocks
below the horizon, and the cloud patches that hang
over every island of the tropic seas, signaling its
presence from afar.

Those who have studied the seafaring of primitive peoples believe that the flight of birds had
much meaning for the Polynesians. It is thought
that they learned much from watching the flocks
that gathered each year in the spring and fall,
launched out over the ocean, and returned later
out of the emptiness into which they had vanished.
Perhaps the Hawaiians found their islands by following the golden plover from Tahiti, as the birds
returned to the North American mainland. Perhaps the shining cuckoo guided other colonists
from the Solomon Islands to New Zealand.

*Knowing that certain stars would pass over the
island they hoped to reach, the Polynesians followed
these stars and sailed on in the clear Pacific night.*

His eyes fixed on the horizon, the Noah of the French cathedral of Bourges releases a land-seeking dove.

Traditions and written records, too, tell us that early navigators carried with them birds which they would let go and follow to land. The frigate bird or man-of-war bird was the one the Polynesians used for this purpose. The raven was used by the Norsemen.

It seems from the ancient Norse writings that the Vikings often drifted for days without knowing where they were. Then they had to rely on the flight of birds to tell them where land lay.

Norse mariners on the way from Norway to Greenland were advised to keep far enough to the south of Iceland to have sight of birds and whales from there.

As for the compass, the first mention we have of the use of it as a guide to mariners is in the twelfth century after Christ. But as much as a hundred years later, scholars were still expressing their doubts about it. Should sailors indeed entrust their lives to an instrument so obviously in-

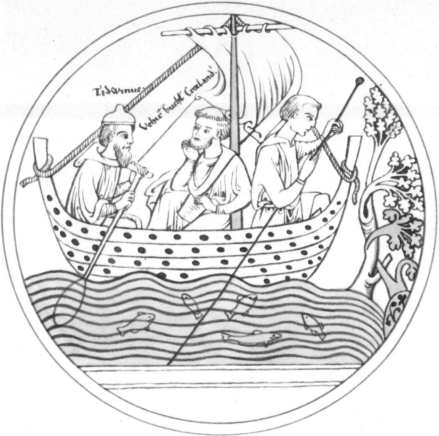

Off on their voyage to Croyland in eastern England, these three men of the Middle Ages seem as big as their sailboat. The steersman, like his Viking counterpart on page 150, holds his steering oar on the starboard side of the boat. The pilot tests the depth with a sounding rod.

Spurred on by a vision of lands beyond the seas, the navigators of the great age of discovery also benefited from several technical innovations. One of these, held in a small box, was the compass; another, clearly visible in this fifteenth century Portuguese plate, was the stern rudder.

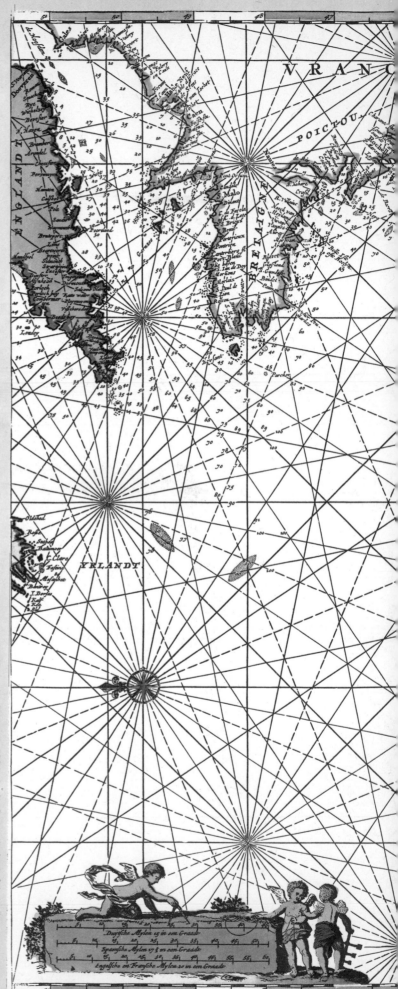

On this chart appear the familiar Atlantic shores of western Europe, from Calais in the upper left corner to Cadiz, to the right. It was published in Amsterdam in the early seventeenth century by Johannes van Keulen, who turned it so that the reader imagined himself facing east, the direction of the Holy Land. He left the inland areas blank, naming only the towns the navigator would see from offshore. But he covered it with lines, and these, to a navigator, were essential. The lines are all part of a system centered on Corunna, the great Spanish harbor from which, in 1588, the Armada had sailed for the coasts of England. From Corunna lines radiate to sixteen points distributed around the map in one large circle; at two of these points a wind rose is surmounted by a fleur-de-lis pointing north. The navigator found the line most nearly parallel to the course between any two points on the chart, then read the correct compass bearing from one of the wind roses.

156

RYCK

Paskaert
Van
CALES tot CADIX
als mede een gedeelte van Engelandt,
Zynde naukeurig opgestelt en veel fouten verbetert door verscheyde
ervaeren Stuer-lieden
't Amsterdam
By Joannes van Keulen Boeck verkooper en
Graed-boogh maecker aan de Nieuw-brug inde
gekroonde Lootsman.
Met Privelegie voor 15 Jaer

Bordeaux

HISPANGIEN

BISCAJJA

GALISIE

GRANADA

PORTUGAJJA

ANDALUZIA

C. de Finisterre

ALGARVE

C. de Gata

Malago

Gibralter

Cadix

Plowing through a heavy sea, a modern schooner relives the adventure of the days of sail.

vented by the devil? But in spite of these fears the compass went on being used in the Mediterranean and spread in the next hundred years to northern Europe.

In the year 1311 Petrus Vesconte made a sea chart. It is the oldest one that has come down to us. But probably there were many charts made before his time. Doubtless they were carefully guarded as secrets of the trade—for the sea charts

were "keys to empire" and a "way to wealth." The mariners of old were not anxious to have it known how they went from place to place. They guarded their secrets carefully.

It was a Dutchman, Lucas Waghenaer by name, who produced the first navigational charts bound together in a book. The *Mariner's Mirror* of Wagnenaer was first published in 1584, and many were the additions to it in later years. In the two

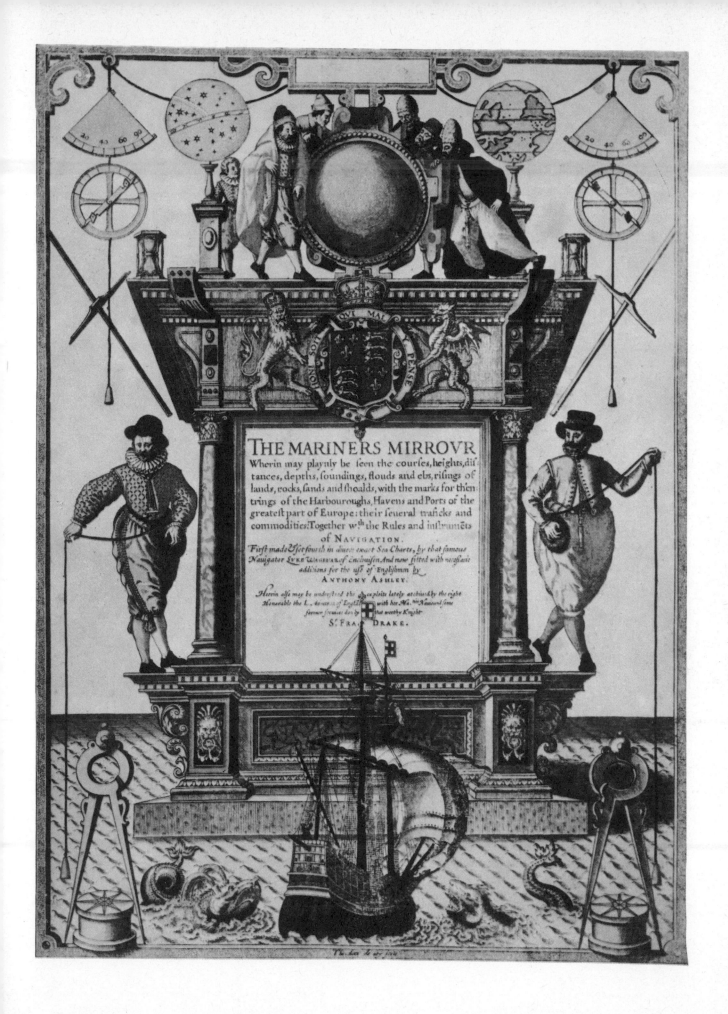

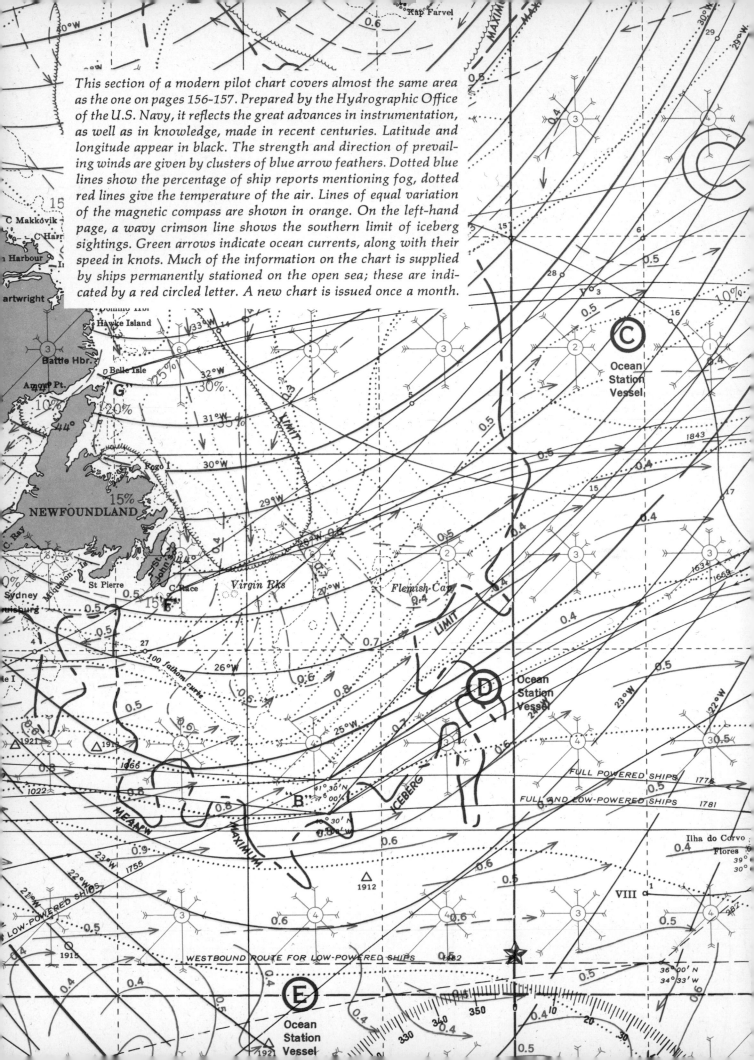

This section of a modern pilot chart covers almost the same area as the one on pages 156-157. Prepared by the Hydrographic Office of the U.S. Navy, it reflects the great advances in instrumentation, as well as in knowledge, made in recent centuries. Latitude and longitude appear in black. The strength and direction of prevailing winds are given by clusters of blue arrow feathers. Dotted blue lines show the percentage of ship reports mentioning fog, dotted red lines give the temperature of the air. Lines of equal variation of the magnetic compass are shown in orange. On the left-hand page, a wavy crimson line shows the southern limit of iceberg sightings. Green arrows indicate ocean currents, along with their speed in knots. Much of the information on the chart is supplied by ships permanently stationed on the open sea; these are indicated by a red circled letter. A new chart is issued once a month.

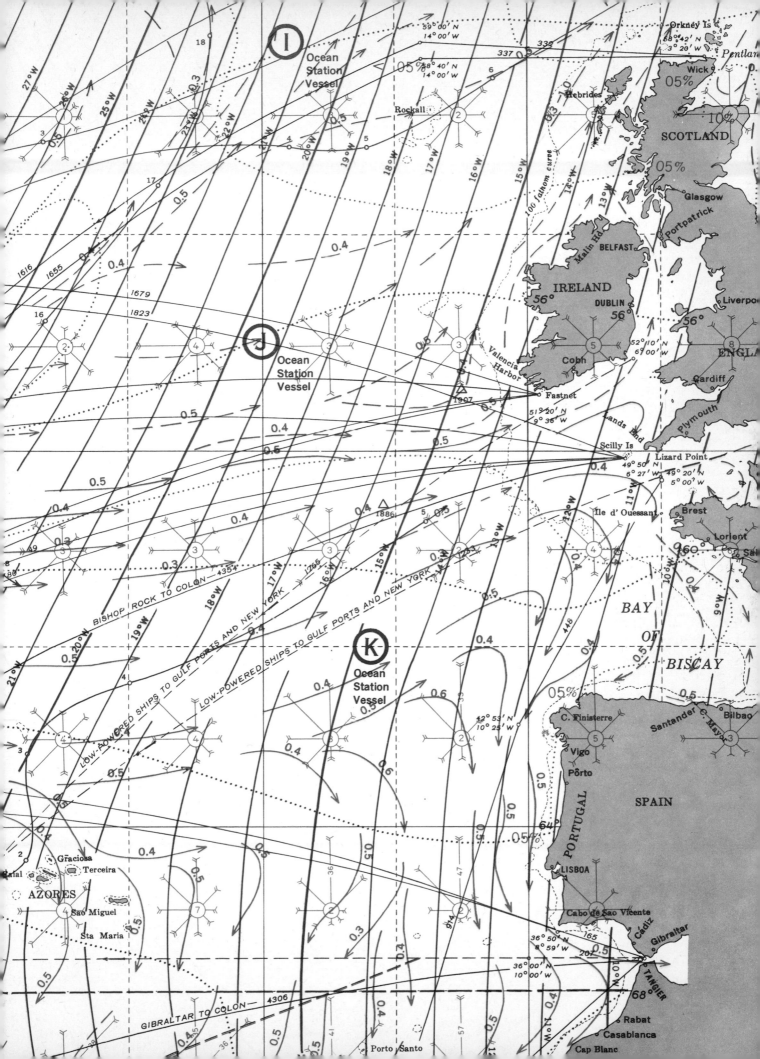

centuries that followed, in the competition for the wealth of the East Indies, the finest charts were prepared not by governments but by the privately run East India companies. For a long time these charts were guarded as one of the most precious secrets of their trade. But when the Company's chart maker became chart maker for the British Navy, Great Britain began to make its own maps and give out the information for the benefit of the world's seafarers.

It was soon after this that a young man joined the United States Navy who was destined to make great strides in banishing the darkness of the sea. He was Lieutenant Matthew Maury. In only a few years Lieutenant Maury was to make his influence felt on navigation all over the world. He organized a world-wide co-operative system. Ships' officers of all nations sent in the logs of their voyages, and from these Maury got all kinds of information which he put on navigational charts. In return, the co-operating mariner got copies of the charts. Soon Maury's sailing directions had the attention of the world. He had shortened the passage for American east-coast vessels to Rio de Janeiro by 10 days, to Australia by 20 days, and around the horn to California by 30 days.

The modern Sailing Directions and Coast Pilots now put out by every seafaring nation of the world are direct descendants of Maury's charts. In these we find the most complete information a navigator can have to guide him over the ocean. Yet in these writings of the sea, it is pleasant to come upon quaint touches that clearly go back to the ancient Norse and Mediterranean seamen. It is surprising, but pleasant, that today's sailing directions should tell mariners how to find out where they are by radio systems such as loran and at the same time counsel them to be guided by the flight of birds and the behavior of whales in making land in foggy weather—just like the Norsemen of a thousand years ago.

After laying her eggs in the coral sand beyond the reach of the tide, a green turtle returns to the sea.

Sometimes the Pilots have no exact information to give. For some remote areas of the sea they can report only what the whalers or sealers or some old-time fisherman has said about this channel or that tidal current. Or they must put in a chart prepared half a century ago by the last vessel to take soundings in the area. Often they must caution the navigator not to proceed without getting information from those having "local knowledge." In phrases like this we get the feel of the unknown and the mysterious that never quite separates itself from the sea.

So here and there, in a few out-of-the-way places, old-time darkness still lingers over the surface of the waters. But it is passing. Most of the length and breadth of the ocean is known, and it is only in speaking of the depths that we can still use the expression Sea of Darkness. It took centuries to chart the surface of the sea. Our progress in picturing the unseen world beneath it seems very rapid by comparison. But even with all our modern instruments for probing and sampling the deep ocean, no one can say that we shall ever know the last, the final, mysteries of the sea.

The ancients believed that the ocean encircled the world. In a larger sense that is true—for the sea lies all about us. The commerce of all lands must cross it. The very winds that move over the lands were cradled there and seek ever to return to it. The continents themselves dissolve and pass to the sea, grain after grain. The rains that rose from the sea return to it again in rivers. All life began there, and after many changes the dead husks of that same life are received again. For all at last return to the sea—to Oceanus, the ocean river, like the ever-flowing stream of time, the beginning and the end.

INDEX